D0397387

The Mind Managers

THE MIND MANAGERS

HERBERT I. SCHILLER

Beacon Press *Boston*

Beacon Press books are published under the auspices
of the Unitarian Universalist Association
Published simultaneously in Canada by Saunders of Toronto, Ltd.

Printed in the United States of America

9 8 7 6 5 4 3 2

A brief section in Chapter 1 appeared originally
as "Social Control and Individual Freedom" in
The Bulletin of the Atomic Scientists, May 1968.
It is reprinted by permission of Science and Public
Affairs, *The Bulletin of the Atomic Scientists*.

A portion of Chapter 3 appeared originally as
"A New Klondike for an Old Complex" in *The Progressive*,
May 1969. It is reprinted with permission of
The Progressive.

A portion of Chapter 5 originally appeared in "Polls
Are Prostitutes for the Establishment," *Psychology
Today* Magazine, July 1972. Copyright © Communications/
Research/Machines, Inc.

A portion of Chapter 6 originally appeared in "Madison
Avenue Imperialism," *Transaction–Society* Magazine, March/April
1971.

A portion of Chapter 7 originally appeared in "Mind
Management: Mass Media in the Advanced Industrial
State," *Quarterly Review of Economics and Business*,
Spring 1971.

Library of Congress Cataloging in Publication Data

Schiller, Herbert I 1919–
The mind managers.
Includes bibliographical references.
1. Mass media–Social aspects–United States.
2. Mass media–United States. I. Title.
HN90.M3S33 301.16'1'0973 73–6248
ISBN 0–8070–0506–1

For Dan and Zach and their friends

Contents

Acknowledgments

In the initial stages of my research, I had the very capable assistance of Corinne Guntzel, Charles Cooper, and Pam Tate Eversole, who were, at different times, my research assistants while I was still at the University of Illinois. Dan Schiller did the bulk of the preparatory research on Chapter 4, Recreation and Entertainment: Reinforcement for the Status Quo.

Old friends and colleagues at the University of Illinois, Professor V. Lewis Bassie and Professor Joseph D. Phillips, carefully read selected chapters. They offered their usual sound advice and wherever I took it the book benefited greatly. Professor Eleanor Blum, Communications Librarian at the University of Illinois, and Anita R. Schiller, reference bibliographer at the University of California, San Diego, provided valuable bibliographic and reference assistance. Mr. Arnold C. Tovell has been an understanding and very helpful editor.

It is appropriate here also to acknowledge the pioneer work of Professor Dallas Smythe, now at the University of Saskatchewan, on so many of the matters with which this work is concerned. I value his counsel and steadfast friendship.

Mrs. Brenda J. Collins, Administrative Assistant to the Communications Program in Third College, University of California, San Diego, typed many chapter drafts with her customary skill, goodwill, and patience.

Most of the material in this book has not been published before. Those portions which have appeared in print have in most instances been incorporated into larger frameworks and brought up to date. I thank the publishers and editors who have granted me permission to utilize these pieces in this book.

Herbert I. Schiller

Introduction

America's media managers create, process, refine, and preside over the circulation of images and information which determine our beliefs and attitudes and, ultimately, our behavior. When they deliberately produce messages that do not correspond to the realities of social existence, the media managers become mind managers. Messages that intentionally create a false sense of reality and produce a consciousness that cannot comprehend or wilfully rejects the actual conditions of life, personal or social, are manipulative messages.

Manipulation of human minds, according to Paulo Freire, "is an instrument of conquest." It is one of the means by which "the dominant elites try to conform the masses to their objectives."[1] By using myths which explain, justify, and sometimes even glamorize the prevailing conditions of existence, manipulators secure popular support for a social order that is not in the majority's long-term real interest. When manipulation is successful, alternative social arrangements remain unconsidered.

Manipulation is not the initial means adopted by ruling elites to maintain social control. As Freire points out, it is only "when the people begin (even naively) to emerge from the historical process" that the rulers resort to manipulation. "Prior to emergence of the people there is no manipulation (precisely speaking), but rather total suppression. When the oppressed are almost completely submerged in reality, it is unnecessary to manipulate them."[2]

Suppression—the total restraint and subjection of the individual—has not been limited to any single geographical or political entity. Over time and across the world, most people have been suppressed by a condition of total impoverishment which presents itself, sometimes accurately, as "nature." More often it is the consequence of unequal social divisions. Until very recently only a handful of countries has enjoyed the happy combination of location, resource sufficiency, and a lucky historical priority which provided the means to escape scarcity and recurrent economic disaster. And even in those relatively favored locations, suppression remained the fate of most of the people until the late eighteenth and early nineteenth centuries.

From the beginning, North America has been a very special case: a rich continent, free of most of the social bonds that fettered Europe and Asia, wrested unconditionally from its original inhabitants by force and deception. It was developed rapidly according to an economic ethic that took centuries to evolve in Western Europe.

Except for the black, brown, yellow, and red people—exceptions that embraced millions—suppression was never the main instrument of social control in North America. It was needed and invoked only on infrequent and generally short-lived occasions. The controllers of the social order since colonial times effectively manipulated the white majority and suppressed the colored minority. As Gore Vidal notes, "Persuading the people to vote against their own best interests has been the awesome genius of the American political elite from the beginning."[3]

To be sure, the very special conditions of American life—the abundant resources of the lightly settled continent, the unimpeded transfer of technical skills from abroad, the absence of traditional political restrictions, and security from armed invasion during the developmental period—have permitted a historically unprecedented physical mobility and significant economic and social advancement for a large portion of the population. Again, these impressive benefits, though distributed relatively widely across the social spectrum, were unavailable or far less generously allotted to the nation's considerable nonwhite and working-class populations. All the same, these very real tangible improvements made the lines of social control and political authority thin or invisible except during cyclical periods of crisis in the system.

Though it is accurate, I believe, to describe the United States as a divided society in which manipulation is one of the chief instruments of control at the disposition of a small governing group of corporate and governmental decision-makers, one cautionary qualification is useful.

The reality of the distinction between "haves" and "have nots" should not be taken to imply a frozen and unbridgeable separation of the two groups, in which the readily identifiable "haves" struggle from one generation to another to maintain their privileged position. This may and, in fact, does occur. Yet it is not a sufficient explanation of the social dynamics at work. It is essential to remember that for many *individuals* the situation may change.

The normal functioning of a market system, founded on private ownership, continuously produces additions to the upper strata, as well as the middle sectors. A fresh supply of new controllers is constantly available. The cast of rulers and ruled can and does change, though not, of course, with the abruptness of a revolutionary overturn. Former order-receivers can become order-givers. Some of the manipulated may find themselves turned manipulators. But note also that this can occur even in a static social structure in which shifts in one direction are offset by opposing changes.

The permanent division of the society into two broad categories of "winners" and "losers" arises and persists as a result of the maintenance, recognition, and, indeed, sanctification of the system of private ownership of productive property and the extension of the ownership principle to all other aspects of human existence. The general acceptance of this arrangement for carrying on social activity makes it inevitable that some prosper, consolidate their success, and join the dominant shapers and molders of the community. The others, the majority, work on as mere conformists, the disadvantaged, and the manipulated; they are manipulated especially to continue to participate, if not wholeheartedly, at least positively, in the established routines. The system gives them a return adequate to achieve some marks of economic status, and manipulation leads them to hope that they might turn these routines to greater personal advantage for themselves or their children.

It is not surprising that manipulation, as an instrument of control, should reach its highest development in the United States. In America, more than anywhere else, the favorable conditions we have briefly noted permit a large fraction of the population to escape total suppression and thereby become potential actors in the historical process. Manipulation allows the appearance of active engagement while denying many of the material and *all* of the psychic benefits of genuine involvement.

Where manipulation is the principal means of social control, as it is in the United States, the articulation and refinement of manipulative techniques take precedence over other intellectual activities. In accordance with market principles, therefore, manipulative work attracts the keenest talent because it offers the system's richest incentives. Talented Ph.D.'s in English literature wind up as advertising copywriters. Madison Avenue pays a lot more than do college English departments.

The means of manipulation are many, but, clearly, control of the informational and ideational apparatus at all levels is essential. This is secured by the operation of a simple rule of the market economy. Ownership and control of the mass media, like all other forms of property, is available to those with capital. Inevitably, radio- and television-station ownership, newspaper and magazine proprietorship, movie-making, and book publishing are largely in the hands of corporate chains and media conglomerates. The apparatus is thus ready to assume an active and dominant role in the manipulative process.

My intention is to identify some of these conditioning forces and to reveal the means by which they conceal their presence, deny their influence, or exercise directional control under auspices that superficially appear benign and/or natural. The search for these "hidden processes," along with their subtle mechanics, should not be mistaken for a more common kind of investigation—the exposé of clandestine activities. Conspiracy is neither invoked nor considered in these pages. Though the idea of mind management lends itself easily to such an approach, the comprehensive conditioning carried on throughout American society today does not require, and actually cannot be understood in, such terms.

Of course, conspiracies and conspirators are at work in the social realm. (How else can one account for the bugging of the Democratic National Headquarters in mid-1972?) Yet these activities, large or small, revealed or still covert, can be accounted for within the deeper realities of the society.

No cultural committee draws up secret instructions for the daily schooling and programming of the American people, although the Nixon Administration does what it can to this end. In truth, the process is much more elusive and far more effective because it generally runs without central direction. It is embedded in the unquestioned but fundamental socioeconomic arrangements that first determine, and then are reinforced by, property ownership, division of labor, sex roles, the organization of production, and the distribution of income. These arrangements, established and legitimized over a very long time, have their own dynamics and produce their own "inevitabilities."

I have attempted to examine some of these inevitabilities and to question their legitimacy. To do this in a thorough and systematic way would demand resources of time, energy, and skill beyond one person's (or at least this person's) command. Accordingly, this book is intended to provide only a sketch, a possible approach by which the information-gathering and information-disseminating processes can be examined critically and their most basic functions understood—in contradiction to what they claim to be doing.

Another consideration that has played a part in this book is the recognition that research about the United States' communications apparatus is of the highest interest to the international community. This is so not only because of the great curiosity about this country abroad, but also because of the vital questions this system poses about national sovereignty and even survival. North American culture is being exported globally. Already it has become the dominant paradigm in many places outside the United States. The announcement of the arrival of Pepsi-Cola in the Soviet Union is the latest symptom of the worldwide advance of North American consumerist ideology.

Understanding the mechanics of the American cultural industry is urgently necessary. The products and artifacts of this industry are made to identifiable specifications and with ascertainable ingredients. Viewers, listeners, and readers, at home and abroad, are well advised to familiarize themselves with these features, but it should be noted that this familiarity can, under certain auspices, be harmful to your (mental) health.

It is only proper that American researchers turn their attention to these matters. It is the least they can do at a time when their own society's governors seem so intent on capturing the minds and souls of peoples everywhere.

Domestically, the mind management industry is enjoying an exceptional growth period. The national election campaign of 1972 provided some previews of what may be ahead in the way of packaging consciousness. Still, it is essential to remember that the techniques of information and image control, so highly developed in present-day Washington, have their antecedents. The fine art of control through persuasion has not just suddenly emerged. A spectacular excursion into mind management, predating the Nixon era by more than two decades, was the successful effort in 1945 to convince the American people that their daily existence was threatened by the war-devastated and totally drained Russian economy. Since then, advances in communications technology have facilitated more sophisticated forms of manipulation.

Now a national communications pageant is orchestrated by the surrogates of the state-capitalist economy, resident in the Executive Offices of the White House and in Madison Avenue public relations and advertising agency offices. As the following chapters suggest, there is good reason to believe that information management will be even more highly organized by media controllers in the years ahead. The flow of information in a complex society is a source of unparalleled power. It is unrealistic to imagine that control of this power will be relinquished readily.

Yet the problems besetting the American corporate economy are enormous and, Dow-Jones breakthroughs notwithstanding, they continue to accumulate. However long their resolution may be postponed, the crunch, when and in whatever form it comes, will be resounding. At that time, the informational system, already so extensive and concentrated, may with astonishing ease serve ends other than those of the corporate interests it represents so unhesitatingly today.

CHAPTER ONE

Manipulation and the Packaged Consciousness

Five Myths That Structure Content

1. *The Myth of Individualism and Personal Choice*

MANIPULATION'S GREATEST TRIUMPH, most observable in the United States, is to have taken advantage of the special historical circumstances of Western development to perpetrate as truth a definition of freedom cast in individualistic terms. This enables the concept to serve a double function. It protects the ownership of productive private property while simultaneously offering itself as the guardian of the individual's well-being, suggesting, if not insisting, that the latter is unattainable without the existence of the former. Upon this central construct an entire scaffolding of manipulation is erected. What accounts for the strength of this powerful notion?

There is evidence enough to argue that the sovereign individual's rights are a myth, and that society and the individual are inseparable. As Lomax and Berkowitz have written, and many others have observed, "the beginnings of culture [were] rooted in cooperation and communication."[1] Yet the basis of freedom as it is perceived in the West is the existence of substantial individual choice. Personal choice has been emphasized as highly desirable and attainable in significant measure. The origin of this sentiment is not recent. The identification of personal choice with human freedom can be seen arising side-by-side with seventeenth-century individualism, both products of the emerging market economy.[2]

For several hundred years individual proprietorship, allied with technological improvement, increased output and thereby bestowed great importance on personal independence in the industrial and political processes. The view that freedom is a personal matter, and that the individual's rights supersede the group's and provide the basis for social organization, gained credibility with the rise of material rewards and leisure time. Note, however, that these conditions were not distributed evenly among all classes of Western society and that they did not begin to exist in the rest of the world.

The success of a new class of entrepreneurs seemingly confirmed the workability and desirability of the institutional changes. Individual choice and private decision-making were, at that time, functional activities—constructive and useful in the achievement of the higher outputs, increased productive efficiency, and soaring profits of the business unit. The solid evidence of economic development and rising output in Western Europe helped the self-serving claims of individualism, personal choice, and private accumulation to take root and flourish.

In the newly settled United States, few restraints impeded the imposition of an individualistic private entrepreneurial system and its accompanying myths of personal choice and individual freedom. Both enterprise and myth found a hospitable setting. The growth of the former and consolidation of the latter were inevitable. How far the process has been carried is evident today in the easy public acceptance of the giant multinational private corporation as an example of individual endeavor.

For example, Frank Stanton, until recently Vice Chairman of CBS, the most important broadcasting conglomerate in the nation, challenges the right of the United Nations to regulate international satellite communications, though satellites may soon make it possible to broadcast messages directly into individual homes anywhere in the world. Stanton asserts that "the rights of Americans to speak to whomever they please, when they please, are bartered away" [through such regulation].[3] Stanton is concerned about CBS' rights to communicate with whomever it pleases. The ordinary American citizen has neither the means nor the facilities to communicate internationally in any significant way.

Privatism in every sphere of life is considered normal. The American life style, from its most minor detail to its most deeply felt beliefs and practices, reflects an exclusively self-centered outlook, which is in turn an accurate image of the structure of the economy itself. The American dream includes a personal means of transportation, a single-family home, the proprietor-operated business. Such other institutions as a competitive health system are obvious, if not natural, features of the privately organized economy.

In this setting, it is to be expected that whatever changes do occur will be effected through individualistic and private organizational means. In the face of the disintegration of urban life, land use remains private. When space communications were developed in the 1960s, offering the potential instrumentation for international social discourse, Comsat, a private corporation with three publicly appointed directors for window dressing, was entrusted with this global responsibility. Though parts of Southern California are practically invisible and smog clouds hang over most American cities, the nation's economy continues to be tied to Detroit production lines and the happy image of the three-car family.

Though individual freedom and personal choice are its most powerful mythic defenses, the system of private ownership and production requires and creates additional constructs, along with the techniques to transmit them. These notions either rationalize its existence and promise a great future, or divert attention from its searing inadequacies and conceal the possibilities of new departures for human development. Some of these constructs and techniques are not exclusive to the privatistic industrial order, and can be applied in any social system intent on maintaining its dominion. Other myths, and the means of circulating them, are closely associated with the specific characteristics of this social system.

2. *The Myth of Neutrality*

For manipulation to be most effective, evidence of its presence should be nonexistent. When the manipulated believe things are the way they are naturally and inevitably, manipulation is successful. In short, manipulation requires a false reality that is a continuous denial of its existence.

It is essential, therefore, that people who are manipulated believe in the neutrality of their key social institutions. They must believe that government, the media, education, and science are beyond the clash of conflicting social interests. Government, and the national government in particular, remains the centerpiece of the neutrality myth. This myth presupposes belief in the basic integrity and nonpartisanship of government in general and of its constituent parts—Congress, the judiciary, and the Presidency. Corruption, deceit, and knavery, when they occur from time to time, are seen to be the result of human weakness. The institutions themselves are beyond reproach. The fundamental soundness of the overall system is assured by the well-designed instrumentalities that comprise the whole.

The Presidency, for instance, is beyond the reach of special interests, according to this mythology. The first and most extreme manipulative use of the Presidency, therefore, is to claim the nonpartisanship of the office, and to seem to withdraw it from clamorous conflict. In the 1972 elections, the Republican candidate campaigned under the auspices and slogans of the Committee to Re-elect the President, not as the flesh and blood Richard M. Nixon.

The chief executive, though the most important, is but one of many governmental departments that seek to present themselves as neutral agents, embracing no objectives but the general welfare, and serving everyone impartially and disinterestedly. For half a century all the media joined in propagating the myth of the FBI as a nonpolitical and highly effective agency of law enforcement. In fact, the Bureau has been used continuously to intimidate and coerce social critics.

The mass media, too, are supposed to be neutral. Departures from evenhandedness in news reportage are admitted but, the press assures us, result from human error and cannot be interpreted as flaws in the basically sound institutions of information dissemination. That the media (press, periodicals, radio, and television) are almost without exception business enterprises, receiving their revenues from commercial sales of time or space, seems to create no problems for those who defend the objectivity and integrity of the informational services.[4] In the Nixon years the media have increasingly been questioned, but only because they have not tilted far enough toward the right.

Science, which more than any other intellectual activity has been integrated into the corporate economy, continues also to insist on its value-free neutrality. Unwilling to consider the implications of the sources of its funding, the directions of its research, the applications of its theories, and the character of the paradigms it creates, science promotes the notion of its insulation from the social forces that affect all other ongoing activities in the nation.

The system of schooling, from the elementary through the university level, is also, according to the manipulators, devoid of deliberate ideological purpose. Still, the product must reflect the teaching: it is astonishing how large a proportion of the graduates at each stage continue, despite all the ballyhoo about the counterculture, to believe in and observe the competitive ethic of business enterprise.

Wherever one looks in the social sphere, neutrality and objectivity are invoked to describe the functioning of value-laden and purposeful activities which lend support to the prevailing institutional system. Essential to the everyday maintenance of the control system is the carefully nurtured myth that no special groups or views have a preponderant influence on the country's important decision-making processes. Conventional economics has long contended that all agents enter the market more or less equal as buyers and sellers, workers and employers, and take their chances in an uncontrolled arena of independent choice-making. Manipulation in market economics is an aberration which everyone abhors and does his best to eliminate, usually by not acknowledging it. Similarly, in the marketplace of ideas, the manipulators insist that there is no ideology that operates as a control mechanism. There is only, they claim, an information-knowledge spectrum, from which the neutral scientist, teacher, government official, or individual picks and chooses the informational bits most useful to the pattern of truth he or she is attempting to construct. Daniel Bell, at the beginning of one of the most spectacular decades of social conflict and manipulative control in the United States' history, published a book proclaiming the "end of ideology."[5]

3. *The Myth of Unchanging Human Nature*

Human expectations can be the lubricant of social change. When human expectations are low, passivity prevails. There can, of course, be various kinds of images in anyone's mind concerning political, social, economic, and personal realities. The common denominator of all such imagery, however, is the view people have of human nature. What human nature is seen to be ultimately affects the way human beings behave, not because they must act as they do but because they believe they are expected to act that way. One writer puts it this way: ". . . the behavior of men is not independent of the theories of human behavior that men adopt . . . what we believe of man affects the behavior of men, for it determines what each expects of the other . . . belief helps shape actuality."[6]

It is predictable that in the United States a theory that emphasizes the aggressive side of human behavior and the unchangeability of human nature would find approval, permeate most work and thought, and be circulated widely by the mass media. Certainly, an economy that is built on and rewards private ownership and individual acquisition, and is subject to the personal and social conflicts these arrangements impose, can be expected to be gratified with an explanation that legitimizes its operative principles. How reassuring to consider these conflictful relationships inherent in the human condition rather than imposed by social circumstance! This outlook fits nicely too with the antiideological stance the system projects. It induces a "scientific" and "objective" approach to the human condition, rigorously measuring human microbehavior in all its depravities, and for the most part ignoring the broader and less measurable social parameters.

Daily TV programming, for example, with its quota of half a dozen murders per hour, is rationalized easily by media controllers as an effort to give the people what they want. Too bad, they shrug, if human nature demands eighteen hours daily of mayhem and slaughter.

The market for the works of authors who explain human aggressiveness and predatoriness by referring to animal behavior is booming. Well it might! No one can avoid encountering almost daily, directly or indirectly, shockingly antihuman behavior. How do the "crisis-managers" of the market economy account for the very visible tears in the social fabric? Consciousness controllers need not intentionally construct explanations that dull awareness and lessen the pressure for social change. The cultural industry, operating according to ordinary competitive principles, will produce any number of explanatory theories. The information machinery will see to it, strictly as a paying proposition, that people have the "opportunity" to read, see, and hear about the latest theory linking urban crime to the mating behavior of carnivores.

Fortune finds it cheering, for example, that some American social scientists are again emphasizing "the intractability of human nature" in their explanations of social phenomena. "The orthodox view of environment as the all-important influence on people's behavior," it reports, "is yielding to a new awareness of the role of hereditary factors: enthusiasm for schemes to reform society by remolding men is giving way to a healthy appreciation of the basic intractability of human nature."[7]

The net social effects of the thesis that human nature is at fault are further disorientation, total inability to recognize the causes of malaise—much less to take any steps to overcome it—and, of most consequence, continued adherence to the *status quo*. It is, precisely, the denial of what one writer describes as "the *human* nature of human nature":

. . . To believe that man's aggressiveness or territoriality is in the nature of the beast is to mistake some men for all men, contemporary society for all possible societies, and, by a remarkable transformation, to justify what is as what needs must be; social repression becomes a response to, rather than a cause of, human violence. Pessimism about man serves to maintain the status quo. It is a luxury for the affluent, a sop to the guilt of the politically inactive, a comfort to those who continue to enjoy the amenities of privilege. Pessimism is too costly for the disenfranchised; they give way to it at the price of their salvation . . . men and women must believe that mankind can become fully human in order for our species to attain its humanity. Restated, a soberly optimistic view of man's potential (based on recognition of mankind's attainments, but tempered by knowledge of its frailties) is a precondition for social action to make actual that which is possible.[8]

It is to prevent social action (and it is immaterial whether the intent is articulated or not) that so much publicity and attention are devoted to every pessimistic appraisal of human potential. If we are doomed forever by our inheritance, there is not much to be done about it. But there is a good reason and a good market for undervaluing human capability. An entrenched social system depends on keeping the popular and, especially, the "enlightened" mind unsure and doubtful about its human prospects.

Among the mind manipulators, human nature doesn't change and neither does the world. Freire observes that ". . . the oppressors develop a series of methods precluding any presentation of the world as a problem and showing it rather as a fixed entity, as something given—something to which men, as mere spectators, must adapt."[9]

This does not necessitate ignoring history. On the contrary, endless recitation of what happened in the past accompanies assertions about how much change is occurring under our very noses. But these are invariably *physical* changes—new means of transportation, air conditioning, space rockets, packaged foods. Mind managers dwell on these matters but carefully refrain from considering changes in social relationships or in the institutional structures that undergird the economy.

Every conceivable kind of futuristic device is canvassed and blueprinted. Yet those who will use these wonder items will apparently continue to be married, raise children in suburban homes, work for private companies, vote for a President in a two-party system, and pay a large portion of their incomes for defense, law and order, and superhighways. The world, except for some glamorous surface redecorations, will remain as it is; basic relationships will not change, because they, like human nature, are allegedly unchangeable. As for those parts of the world that have undergone far-reaching social rearrangements, reports of these transformations, if there are any, emphasize the defects, problems, and crises, which are seized upon with relish by domestic consciousness manipulators.

If favorable reports do appear, they are "balanced" by negative appraisals which restore the "proper" and familiar perspective. On the rare occasions when films of Cuba or China, for example, appear on domestic television screens, a reporter's commentary carefully guides the viewer to the "correct" interpretations of what is being seen. Otherwise, it would be unsettling to the customary ways of thought so diligently cultivated in all our informational channels.

4. *The Myth of the Absence of Social Conflict*

Concentrating on the blemishes of revolutionary societies is but one side—the international side—of mind management's undertakings to veil from the public the realities of domination and exploitation.

Consciousness controllers, in their presentation of the domestic scene, deny absolutely the presence of social conflict. On the face of it, this seems an impossible task. After all, violence is "as American as apple pie." Not only in fact but in fantasy: in films, on TV, and over the radio, the daily quota of violent scenarios offered the public is staggering. How is this carnival of conflict reconcilable with the media managers' intent to present an image of social harmony? The contradiction is easily resolved.

As presented by the national message-making apparatus, conflict is almost always an *individual* matter, in its manifestations and in its origin. The social roots of conflict just do not exist for the cultural-informational managers. True, there are "good guys" and "bad guys," but, except for such ritualized situations as westerns, which are recognized as scenarios of the past, role identification is divorced from significant social categories.

Black, brown, yellow, red, and other ethnic Americans have always fared poorly in the manufactured cultural imagery. Still, these are minorities which all segments of the white population have exploited in varying degrees. As for the great social division in the nation, between worker and owner, with rare exceptions it has been left unexamined. Attention is diverted elsewhere—generally toward the problems of the upward-striving middle segment of the population, that category with which everyone is supposed to identify.

An unwillingness to recognize and explain the deepest conflict situation in the social order is no recent development in the performance of the cultural-informational apparatus. It has been standard operating procedure from the beginning. Authentic cultural creation that recognizes this reality is rarely encountered in the mass of material that flows through the national informational circuitry. In fact, the banality of most programming, especially that which concerns momentous social events, is attributable to the media's institutional inability to accept and identify the bases of social conflict. It is not an oversight, nor is it an indication of creative ineptitude. It is the result of an intentional policy which most cultural controllers accept without reluctance.

Elite control requires omission or distortion of social reality. Honest examination and discussion of social conflict can only deepen and intensify resistance to social inequity. Economically powerful groups and companies quickly get edgy when attention is called to exploitative practices in which they are engaged. *Variety*'s television editor, Les Brown, described such an incident. Coca-Cola Food Company and the Florida Fruit and Vegetable

Association reacted sharply to a TV documentary, "Migrant," which centered on migrant fruit pickers in Florida. Brown wrote that "the miracle of *Migrant* was that it was televised at all." Warnings were sent to NBC not to show the program because it was "biased." Cuts in the film were demanded, and at least one was made. Finally, after the showing, "Coca-Cola shifted all its network billings to CBS and ABC."[10]

On a strictly commercial level, the presentation of social issues creates uneasiness in mass audiences, or so the audience researchers believe. To be safe, to hold onto as large a public as possible, sponsors are always eager to eliminate potentially "controversial" program material.

The entertainments and cultural products that have been most successful in the United States, those that have received the warmest support and publicity from the communications system, are invariably movies, TV programs, books, and mass entertainments (i.e., Disneyland) which may offer more than a fair quota of violence but never take up *social* conflict. As Freire writes, ". . . concepts such as unity, organization and struggle are immediately labeled as dangerous. In fact, of course, these concepts *are* dangerous—to the oppressors—for their realization is necessary to actions of liberation."[11]

When, in the late 1960s, social conflict erupted and protests against the Vietnamese war and demonstrations for social change became almost a daily occurrence, the communications system was briefly confounded. It recovered its poise quickly, and before the end of the decade a flood of "youth" movies, and films with "black" scenarios were rushed onto the nation's screens. "Shaft," "Super-Fly," "Black Gunn," and "Hit Man," termed "Modern Nigger-Toys" by Imamu Amiri Baraka, are good business. They fulfill Jim Brown's injunction to black film-makers: "The one approach that will work is to approach movies as an industry, as a business. Black people must stop crying '*Black*' and start crying '*Business*.' "[12] Such cultural items, it need hardly be said, offer little illumination of root causes but make up for their omission with plenty of surface action.

5. *The Myth of Media Pluralism*

Personal choice exercised in an environment of cultural-informational diversity is the image, circulated worldwide, of the condition of life in America. This view is also internalized in the belief structure of a large majority of Americans, which makes them particularly susceptible to thoroughgoing manipulation. It is, therefore, one of the central myths upon which mind management flourishes. Choice and diversity, though separate concepts, are in fact inseparable; choice is unattainable in any real sense without diversity. If real options are nonexistent, choosing is either meaningless or manipulative. It is manipulative when accompanied by the illusion that the choice is meaningful.

Though it cannot be verified, the odds are that the illusion of informational choice is more pervasive in the United States than anywhere else in the world. The illusion is sustained by a willingness, deliberately maintained by information controllers, to mistake *abundance of media* for *diversity of content*. It is easy to believe that a nation that has 6,700 commercial radio stations, more than 700 commercial TV stations, 1,500 daily newspapers, hundreds of periodicals, a film industry that produces a couple of hundred new features a year, and a billion-dollar private book-publishing industry provides a rich variety of information and entertainment to its people.

The fact of the matter is that, except for a rather small and highly selective segment of the population who know what they are looking for and can therefore take advantage of the massive communications flow, most Americans are basically, though unconsciously, trapped in what amounts to a no-choice informational bind. Variety of opinion on foreign and domestic news or, for that matter, local community business, hardly exists in the media. This results essentially from the inherent identity of interests, material and ideological, of property-holders (in this case, the private owners of the communications media), and from the monopolistic character of the communications industry in general.

The limiting effects of monopoly are in need of no explanation, and communications monopolies restrict informational choice wherever they operate. They offer one version of reality—their own. In this category fall most of the nation's newspapers, magazines, and films, which are produced by national or regional communications conglomerates. The number of American cities in which competing newspapers circulate has shrunk to a handful.

While there is a competition of sorts for audiences among the three major TV networks, two conditions determine the limits of the variety presented. Though each network struggles gamely to attract as large an audience as possible, it imitates its two rivals in program format and content. If ABC is successful with a western serial, CBS and NBC will in all likelihood "compete" with "shoot-'em-ups" in the same time slot. Besides, each of the three national networks is part of, or is itself, an enormous communications business, with the drives and motivations of any other profit-seeking enterprise. This means that diversity in the informational-entertainment sector exists only in the sense that there are a number of superficially different versions of the main categories of program. For example, there are several talk shows on late-night TV; there may be half a dozen private-eye, western, or law-and-order TV serials to "choose from" in prime time; there are three network news commentators with different personalities who offer essentially identical information. One can switch the radio dial and get round-the-clock news from one or, at most, two news services; or one can hear Top 40 popular songs played by "competing" disc jockeys.

Though no single program, performer, commentator, or informational bit is necessarily identical to its competitors, *there is no significant qualitative difference*. Just as a supermarket offers six identical soaps in different colors and a drugstore sells a variety of brands of aspirin at different prices, disc jockeys play the same records between personalized advertisements for different commodities.

The media mix varies in abundance from city to city, and from urban to rural communities. The major metropolitan centers may have half a dozen TV channels, thirty or forty radio stations, two or three newspapers, and dozens of movie houses. Less urbanized communities will ordinarily have far fewer informational-entertainment facilities. The greater the number of communications sources, obviously, the larger the number of informational messages and stimuli. But whether richly or poorly supplied, the result is basically the same. The entertainment, the news, the information, and the messages are selected from the same informational universe by "gatekeepers" motivated by essentially inescapable commercial imperatives. Style and metaphor may vary, but not the essence.

Yet it is this condition of communicational pluralism, empty as it is of real diversity, which affords great strength to the prevailing system of consciousness-packaging. The multichannel communications flow creates confidence in, and lends credibility to, the notion of free informational choice. Meanwhile, its main effect is to provide continuous reinforcement of the *status quo*. Similar stimuli, emanating from apparently diverse sources, envelop the listener/viewer/reader in a message/image environment that ordinarily seems uncontrolled, relatively free, and quite natural. How could it be otherwise with such an abundance of programs and transmitters? Corporate profit-seeking, the main objective of conglomeratized communications, however real and ultimately determining, is an invisible abstraction to the consumers of the cultural images. And one thing is certain: the media do not call their audiences' attention to its existence or its mode of operation.

Writing in *Scientific American,* George Gerbner has observed that "the real question is not whether the organs of mass communication are free but rather: by whom, how, for what purposes and with what consequences are the inevitable controls exercised?"[13]

Looking behind the façade of choice, the television editor of *Variety* addressed himself to a couple of these fundamental questions:

One of the myths about American television is that it operates as a cultural democracy, wholly responsible to the will of the viewing majority in terms of the programs that survive or fade. More aptly, in the area of entertainment mainly, it is a cultural oligarchy, ruled by a consensus of the advertising community. As it happens, television's largest advertisers—the manufacturers of foodstuffs, drugs, beverages, household products, automobiles, cosmetics, and, until 1971, cigarettes, among others—have from the first desired great circulation among the middle classes, so that the density of viewers has become the most important criterion in the evaluation of programs. This emphasis on the popularity of shows has made television appear to be democratic in its principles of program selection. In truth, programs of great popularity go off the air, without regard for the viewers' bereavement, if the kinds of people it reaches are not attractive to advertisers.[14]

The fundamental similarity of the informational material and cultural messages that each of the mass media *independently* transmits makes it necessary to view the communications system as a totality. The media are mutually and continuously reinforcing. Since they operate according to commercial rules, rely on advertising, and are tied tightly to the corporate economy, both in their own structure and in their relationships with sponsors, the media constitute an industry, not an aggregation of independent, freewheeling informational entrepreneurs, each offering a highly individualistic product. By need and by design, the images and messages they purvey, are, with few exceptions, constructed to achieve similar objectives, which are, simply put, profitability and the affirmation and maintenance of the private-ownership consumer society.

Consequently, research directed at discovering the impact of a single TV program or movie, or even an entire category of stimuli, such as "violence on TV," can often be fruitless. Who can justifiably claim that TV violence is inducing delinquent juvenile behavior when violence is endemic to all mass communications channels? Who can suggest that any single category of programming is producing male chauvinist or racist behavior when stimuli and imagery carrying such sentiments flow unceasingly through all the channels of transmission?

It is generally agreed that television is the most powerful

medium; certainly its influence as a purveyor of the system's values cannot be overstated. All the same, television, no matter how powerful, itself depends on the absence of dissonant stimuli in the other media. Each of the informational channels makes its unique contribution, but the result is the same—the consolidation of the *status quo*.

The use of repetition and reinforcement in *all* the media is sometimes admitted in curious, backhanded ways. For example, one of the nation's most influential weekly publications, TV *Guide* (which is examined in some detail in Chapter Four), offers some instructive insights while complaining bitterly about what it terms the negative images of the United States appearing on Western European home screens. In an article entitled "Through A Glass—*very* darkly," Robert Musel writes:

In Monaco earlier this year [*1971*], *I talked to Frank Shakespeare, head of the U.S. Information Agency, about the European view of the United States and the part played in it by "frames of reference." This simply means that an item about America doesn't necessarily give the same impression to a European that it does to an American. From his birth the American absorbs, consciously and unconsciously, a continuous flow of information about his country, and its people, and this is "the frame of reference" which should enable him to evaluate, say, an opportunist radical crying woe about the homeland. The European does not have this background. He sees only a well-known American writer or public figure or film star probably mourning the alleged twilight of democracy in the U.S. And he finds it convincing.*[15]

What the writer is telling us, obliquely, is that most Americans have a reliable "frame of reference," organized "consciously and unconsciously" by communications sources such as TV *Guide*, among hundreds of others. So fortified, the average American will accept information which affirms the consumer society and reject material which views it critically. When an American has been properly "prepared," he or she is relatively invulnerable to dissonant messages, however accurate they may be.[16] No doubt the "frame of reference" would be less effective if communications were in fact pluralistic, as they claim to be, and their messages actually diverse. But with multimedia reinforcement achieved through numerous but only superficially differing informational means, most people's consciousness is neatly packaged from infancy.

The myths we have been describing make up the content of the manipulative system. Let us consider briefly the form of that system.

Two Techniques That Shape Consciousness

1. *Fragmentation as a Form of Communication*

Myths are used to dominate people. When they are inserted unobtrusively into popular consciousness, as they are by the cultural-informational apparatus, their strength is great because most individuals remain unaware that they have been manipulated. The process of control is made still more effective by the special form in which the myth is transmitted. The technique of transmission can in itself add an extra dimension to the manipulative process. What we find, in fact, is that *the form of the communication, as developed in market economies, and in the United States in particular, is an actual embodiment of consciousness control.* This is most readily observed in the technique of information dissemination, used pervasively in America, which we shall term *fragmentation.* Employing a different terminology, Freire observes, "One of the characteristics of oppressive cultural action which is almost never perceived by the dedicated but naive professionals who are involved is the emphasis on a *focalized* view of problems rather than on seeing them as dimensions of a *totality.*"[17]

Fragmentation, or focalization, is the dominant—indeed, the exclusive—format for information and news distribution in North America. Radio and television news is characterized by the machine-gun-like recitation of numerous unrelated items. Newspapers are multipaged assemblages of materials set down almost randomly, or in keeping with arcane rules of journalism. Magazines deliberately break up articles, running the bulk of the text in the back of the issue, so that readers must turn several pages of advertising copy to continue reading. Radio and television programs are incessantly interrupted to provide commercial breaks. The commercial has become so deeply internalized in American viewing/listening life that children's programs, which, it is claimed, are specially designed for educational objectives, utilize the rapid-paced, interrupted pattern of commercial TV though there is no solid evidence that children have short attention spans and need continuous breaks.[18] In fact, it may be that the gradual expansion of the attention span is a controlling factor in the development of children's intelligence. All the same, *Sesame Street*, the widely acclaimed program for youngsters, is in its delivery style indistinguishable from the mind-jarring adult commercial review shows upon which it must base its format or lose its audience of children *already conditioned by commercial programs*.

Fragmentation in information delivery is intensified by the needs of the consumer economy to fill all communications space with commercial messages. Exhortations to buy assail everyone from every possible direction. Subways, highways, the airwaves, the mail, and the sky itself (sky-writing), are vehicles for advertising's unrelenting offensives. The total indifference with which advertising treats any political or social event, insisting on intruding no matter what else is being presented, reduces all social phenomena to bizarre and meaningless happenings. Advertising, therefore, in addition to its already recognized functions of selling goods, fostering new consumer wants, and glamorizing the system, provides still another invaluable service to the corporate economy. Its intrusion into every informational and recreational channel reduces the already minimal capability of audiences to gain a sense of the totality of the event, issue, or subject being presented.

It would be a mistake, however, to believe that without advertising, or with a reduction in advertising, events would receive the holistic treatment that is required for understanding the complexities of modern social existence. Advertising, in seeking benefits for its sponsors, is serendipitous to the system in that its utilization heightens fragmentation.

Yet it is utterly naive to imagine that the informational machinery, the system's most vital lever of domination, would deliberately reveal how domination operates. Consider, for example, the make-up of any ordinary TV or radio news program, or the first page of any major daily newspaper. The feature common to each is the complete heterogeneity of the material and the absolute denial of the relatedness of the social phenomena reported. Talk shows, which proliferate in the broadcasting media, are perfect models of fragmentation as a format. The occasional insertion of a controversial subject or individual in a multi-item program totally defuses, as well as trivializes, controversy. Whatever is said is swallowed up in subsequent commercials, gags, bosoms, and gossip. Yet the matter doesn't end there. Programs of this nature are extolled as evidence of the system's freewheeling tolerance. The media and their controllers boast of the openness of the communications system that permits such critical material to be aired to the nation. Mass audiences accept this argument and are persuaded that they have access to a free flow of opinion.

One of the methods of science that is validly transferable to human affairs is the ecological imperative of recognizing interrelatedness. When the totality of a social issue is deliberately evaded, and random bits pertaining to it are offered as "information," the results are guaranteed: at best, incomprehension; ignorance, apathy, and indifference for the most part.

The mass media are by no means alone in accentuating fragmentation. The entire cultural-educational sphere encourages and promotes atomization, specialization, and microscopic compartmentalization. A university course catalogue listing departmental offerings in the social sciences reveals the arbitrary separations enforced in the university learning process. Each discipline insists on its own purity, and the models most admired in each field are those that exclude the untidy effects of interaction with other disciplines. Economics is for economists; politics is for political scientists. Though the two are inseparable in the world of reality, academically their relationship is disavowed or disregarded.

When the Secretary of Commerce went to Moscow in the summer of 1972 to try to negotiate a major trade agreement with the Russians, the negotiations were stalled because the United States wanted the Russians, as a prior condition to the agreement, to bring pressure on the North Vietnamese to stop fighting. As Secretary of Commerce Peter G. Peterson admitted, "There is a relationship between economics and politics."[19] Try to find such connections in school economics texts that discuss trade, economic aid, development, and productivity.

An additional dimension of fragmentation is achieved when the informational system avails itself of the new communications technology. The flow of disconnected information is speeded up and, with some justification, complaints about "information overload" increase. Actually, there is no excess of *meaningful* information. Just as advertising disrupts concentration and renders trivial the information it interrupts, the new and efficient technology of information-handling permits the transmission of torrents of irrelevant information, further undermining the individual's almost hopeless search for meaning.

2. *Immediacy of Information*

Closely associated with fragmentation and, in fact, a necessary element in its operation, is *immediacy*. This here-and-now quality helps increase the manipulatory power of the informational system. That the information is evanescent, with hardly any enduring structure, also undermines understanding. Still, instantaneousness—the reporting of events as soon after their occurrence as possible—is one of the most revered principles of American journalism. Those social systems that do not provide instantaneous information are regarded either as hopelessly backward and inefficient or—a much more serious charge—as socially delinquent.

But speed of delivery is hardly a virtue in itself. In America, the competitive system transforms news events into commodities, and advantage can be realized by being the first to acquire and dispose of this perishable commodity, the news. The case of Jack Anderson, a highly successful columnist with many well-publicized news coups to his credit, is illustrative. He could not resist going on the air with undocumented charges against Thomas Eagleton, who was fighting to remain on the 1972 Democratic ticket as the candidate for Vice-President. Confronted with the inaccuracy of his information, after maximum damage had been done to Eagleton, Anderson apologized by blaming "the competitive situation." If he hadn't jumped the gun, someone else would have beaten him to it.[20]

Utilizing modern electronics and propelled by competitive drives, information dissemination in the United States and other Western societies is carried on most of the time in an atmosphere of pressure and tension. When there is a genuine or even a psuedo crisis, a hysterical and frenzied atmosphere totally unconducive to reason is created. The false sense of urgency generated by the insistence on immediacy tends to inflate, and subsequently deflate, the importance of all subject matter. Consequently, the ability to discriminate between different degrees of significance is impaired. The rapid-fire announcement of a plane crash, an NLF offensive in Vietnam, a local embezzlement, a strike, and a heat wave, defies assessment and judgment. This being so, the mental sorting-out process that would ordinarily assist in creating meaning is abandoned. The mind becomes a sieve, through which dozens of announcements, a few important but most insignificant, are poured almost hourly. Information, rather than helping to focus awareness and create meaning, results instead in a subliminal recognition of inability to deal with the waves of events that keep breaking against one's consciousness, which in self-defense must continuously lower its threshold of sensitivity.

In New York City, for example, the next day's newspapers are available at 10:30 P.M. The importance of tomorrow's newspaper is that it makes perishable what happened today. Having disposed of today, life moves on to the next cluster of unrelated episodes. Yet most events of significance mature over a considerable period of time. Understanding these developments is not facilitated by 90-second news flashes relayed by space satellites. Total preoccupation with the moment destroys necessary links with the past.

The technology that permits and facilitates immediacy of information is not at issue. It exists and could, under different conditions, be useful. What is of concern is the present social system's utilization of the techniques of rapid communications delivery to blur or eradicate meaning while claiming that such speed enhances understanding and enlightenment. The corporate economy misapplies the techniques of modern communication. As presently employed, communication technologies transmit ahistorical and, therefore, antiinformational messages.

It is easy to imagine electronic formats that would use instantaneousness as a supplement to the construction of meaningful contexts. It is not so easy to believe that immediacy, *as a manipulative device*, will be abandoned while it serves mind managers by effectively preventing popular comprehension and understanding.

Passivity: The Ultimate Objective of Mind Management

The content and form of American communications—the myths and the means of transmitting them—are devoted to manipulation. When successfully employed, as they invariably are, the result is individual passivity, a state of inertia that precludes action. This, indeed, is the condition for which the media and the system-at-large energetically strive, because passivity assures the maintenance of the *status quo*. Passivity feeds upon itself, destroying the capacity for social action that might change the conditions that presently limit human fulfillment. It is appropriate, in this respect, that the group that is challenging the content of children's programs on commercial television, calls itself *Action* for Children's Television [emphasis mine].

In the advanced market economy, passivity has a physical and an intellectual dimension, both of which are skillfully exploited by the techniques and the messages of the mind management machinery.

Television is only the latest and most effective instrument for inducing individual passivity. The statistics on TV-viewing are, in themselves, paralyzing. Americans spend hundreds of millions of hours a week, billions of hours a year, before the set without the slightest encouragement to move out of the living room. Yet far more is involved than the massive physical inactivation of scores of millions of bodies. The diminution of mental activity, the outcome of endless hours of mind-dulling programming, is incalculable. Equally unmeasurable but of enormous import is the pacifying effect on critical consciousness. As Rudolph Arnheim describes it,

One of the characteristic things about television is that you turn it on and then you take whatever comes, which implies an enormously passive attitude on the part of the viewer. It doesn't matter what is coming out of this thing—it may be a foreign language program, maybe something no one has any interest in. And a stimulation to which you're not really responding will put you to sleep. It's as if someone were petting you . . . something that does not stimulate you, does not provoke you to react, but simply eliminates the necessity to be mentally active. Your brain is kept busy in a noncommittal fashion. The senses, which otherwise would be under the obligation to do something active, are occupied.[21]

To be sure, the corporate economy does not rely exclusively on television to spread passivity. Before television, there were diversions enough with similar awareness-reducing effects. Radio, the movies, mass spectator sports, parades, and a large variety of lesser events have made and continue to make their contribution to de-energizing human reactions.

Though most of these entertainments demand nonparticipation, in the physical sense at least, there is nothing inherent in radio, television, or film—to take the most important of the popular recreational arts—that inevitably and exclusively creates mental torpor. There are, of course, infrequent examples of broadcasts that have heightened awareness and focused attention on matters of extreme relevance. But these exceptions cannot conceal the main point: that the *aim* of television and radio programming and films in a commercial society is not to arouse but to lessen concern about social and economic realities.

Furthermore, action is quickly taken to insure that exceptions are no more than that. Fred Friendly has documented his run-ins with the CBS directorate in the 1950s, when he and Edward R. Morrow were producing their critical documentaries.[22] The Smothers Brothers too discovered how short their leash was when they tugged too hard by taking a few mild digs at the Establishment on their program. Their show was terminated summarily.

Much of the informational machinery, in its technological aspects, has a tendency to generate passivity. It is all too easy to switch on a dial, sink back into a sofa, and allow images to pass without mediation into the mind. When this tendency of the communications hardware is supplemented by packaged programming that deliberately seeks the same paralyzing effect, the result is usually stupefying. Writing about the American newsreel in its heyday, in terms totally applicable to the 1970s, one reviewer observed: ". . . the American newsreel gave audiences football games, floods, bathing beauties and celebrities. The movie-goer of the 1930's would learn far more about John Dillinger or Miss America than about the Little Steel Strike or the Spanish Civil War."[23]

The lethal combination of intentionally devitalized programming and physically inactivating communications technology is the machinery of contemporary American mind management. Creative efforts to overcome, or at least counterbalance, this passivity-inducing system are desperately needed. An imaginative approach can promote participation and awareness, but it is unrealistic to expect the corporate economy to encourage such efforts. In any event, the first task, which may be approached modestly, is to comprehend the manipulative function in its many manifestations in the informational arts. Let us examine some of the specifics of this manipulation.

CHAPTER TWO

The Knowledge Industry: The Governmental Component

I signed this measure [the Freedom of Information Act] with a deep sense of pride that the United States is an open society in which the people's right to know is cherished and guarded.

LYNDON B. JOHNSON

GOVERNMENTS MAKE INFORMATION and produce knowledge as natural byproducts of the many functions in which they are engaged. The information and knowledge produced ordinarily reflect the functions undertaken.

The growth of government, for whatever reasons, increases its informational output. Information in incredible amounts and of all sorts funnels into the many branches of the United States Government. There are, for example, data on people, production, natural resources, relations between nations, and other categories of information too numerous to list. The range of subjects covered and the details of coverage are overwhelming when presented in quantitative terms. The United States Government Printing Office, for instance, receives twenty railroad carloads of paper daily, fueling a printing operation that costs $200 million annually.[1]

The Clearinghouse for Federal Scientific and Technical Information houses "millions of copies of over 600,000 separate research reports, to which 50,000 new titles are added each year." These reports, which are for sale, are some of the results of federally supported technological research. And there are additional government information depots, such as the Defense Documentation Center and "more than fifty agencies and departments with major research programs."[2]

Yet the size of the informational output, though interesting as a "piece of information," obscures more than it reveals. The fact that the Government Printing Office is the world's largest publisher offers few clues to the origin and character of the information published for public consumption, or, perhaps more significantly, of that published for limited distribution.

To be sure, the quantity of information bears a close connection to the size of the national administrative apparatus, but it is the kind of governmental activity undertaken that is the decisive factor in the content and social utility of the information generated. Or, stated differently, what the government is *doing* determines the kind of information it is seeking and disseminating. And what the government is doing can best be understood by focusing on the economic system it serves and administers.

The interrelatedness of economic and social processes requires an increasing amount of coordination to assure human and environmental survival, if not improvement. For most people this involves such arrangements as income maintenance, educational support, health and old age security, and numerous other basic amenities. For the environment this means town planning, transport organization, communications development, and resource utilization. All of these matters are, or should be, important concerns of government. The extent to which government seriously addresses itself to these enormously complex yet very immediate matters is as good an index as we have of its social responsiveness to the needs of the people. In an advanced industrial society, the role of government will be large; but the precise dimensions of that role and in whose interest it will be performed depend greatly on the structure and thrust of the overall economy.

Underpinning American society is an industrial system that is privately owned, corporately organized, governmentally protected, and internationally based. The most influential corporations have plants and subsidiaries in dozens of countries. American troops are garrisoned around the world, claiming to protect other nations against communism but actually serving as defenders of these far-flung corporate interests. Secretary of State William P. Rogers, concerned about criticism of American foreign policy, described, with the customary euphemisms, the material basis of the country's international diplomacy: "We have 60 per cent of the direct foreign investment in the world. We're involved all over the world. It's natural for Americans to be involved and we have to be, whether we like it or not, so any tendency toward isolationism, I think, is a dangerous one."[3]

American enterprise is now heavily dependent on foreign raw materials for production and on foreign markets for a large portion of its sales. Profitability is the motivating mechanism that keeps the system in motion at home and abroad. These are the salient characteristics of advanced corporate capitalism, and they are most visible in the United States. It is in relation to these determining factors that the informational activities of the federal bureaucracy can be best understood.

The production and control of information at the national level is largely devoted to meeting the needs and extending the influence and credibility of this system. For this reason, the fullest development of state capitalism—the collaboration of the power of the state with the operations of the private economic system—finds expression in the educational–scientific–communications sector. In this area the dividing lines between public and private spheres are largely erased, and the mutual interpenetration of business and government is most pronounced. Indeed, the administrative apparatus of the state is almost inseparable from the leading private power nuclei in the communications–information sector. As the newly appointed president of the nation's most powerful broadcasting corporation and general information conglomerate declared, upon assuming his post in 1972: "One of the things that attracted me to CBS was its involvement with the governmental life of the nation."[4]

The state's involvement with the creation and distribution of information and knowledge is, therefore, no less a corporate–military involvement. *Variety*, one of the very few publications that concerns itself with such matters, publishes a frequent "roundup of broadcasters as Government partners in war and peace." A roundup in mid-1972 found that "major national news media [are] still in the incredible paradox of being deeply enmeshed in hard cash (billions of dollars) partnerships with a Government actively and outspokenly. . . . seeking to suppress criticism of the Administration or critical reporting thereon." For example, "Westinghouse (whose subsidiary's Group W), General Tire and Rubber (RKO General) and Avco are all anti-personnel weapons makers . . . General Electric produces Vulcan 20m automatic machine guns and pods for Air Force use . . . CBS Labs was contracted to develop improved quantum efficiency lasar detectors—'sniffers' that pinpoint human and lower animal life in the Vietnam jungle for the bombers."[5]

The information generated by the state reflects the motivations, inclinations, and requirements of the system itself, which moves its requests through the bureaucratic processes of government. The mechanics of these intricate, and by no means centrally directed, maneuvers are visible in the various roles the government assumes in its pursuit of information and in the encouragement it offers to its creation. The state is a handsome subsidizer of information production. At the same time it is an educator of significant proportions. It is engaged heavily in its own press agentry. It operates a global machine for the indoctrination and persuasion of foreign populations. And it decides, not entirely irrationally given the premises of its major concerns, which of the items in its informational storehouse should be released to the public, in what manner, over what time period, and in what dosages. Let us examine, one at a time, these different informational roles of the United States Government.

The Government as a Producer and Collector of Information

It is unlikely that the federal government has developed anything that remotely resembles a national policy on the production and collection of knowledge and information, although it created a Council for Government Communications Policy and Planning in mid-1972.[6] For one thing, the subject is vast and intersects many competing sectors of government. For another, the government—not unlike the private economy and, in fact, reflecting it—is a poorly coordinated apparatus, more inclined to fragmentation and unitized responsibility than to an overall system of decision-making and comprehensive perspectives. Moreover, what knowledge and information are, and why they should be pursued, are awkward questions that the top bureaucracy might just as soon leave unasked.

The absence of a recognizable and neatly articulated national information policy does not mean, however, that the decisions of several influential sources in the bureaucracy do not result in a few clearly identifiable directions. Not surprisingly, these directions—however they originate in the administrative apparatus—are by and large consistent with the motivations and thrust of the corporate economy.

Government spending for research and development—the systematic search for *certain kinds* of information—is a major case in point. The curve of expenditures in this area has arched upward dramatically in the last fifteen years, leveling off somewhat recently. Most of the federal expenditures have been channeled through private industry. Of the more than fifteen billion dollars devoted to research by the national government in 1970, more than half was spent in private industrial labs and enterprises. Less than one-quarter supported federal in-house research.[7]

This pattern of expenditure strengthens the private sector with public funds. More consequential still, the possibility of developing alternative courses for economic growth is weakened because the government's ability to make an independent assessment of a new technology, a new product, or a different general perspective is either poor or nonexistent.

For example, the total annual budget of the National Bureau of Standards, a branch of the Department of Commerce, is about $50 million, whereas the annual research and development expenditures of one major corporation, International Business

Machines (IBM), the computer colossus, is roughly ten times as much. Could the social performance of IBM be monitored by such a puny federal research agency, if it were charged with doing so (which it isn't)? The consciously imposed feebleness of public authority makes it inevitable that corporate perspectives and standards govern the country's technological decision-making and orientation. Small wonder, then, that in 1972 the director of the National Bureau of Standards resigned to become vice-president and chief scientist of IBM.[8]

The super-corporations benefit in other ways from the prevailing pattern of federal research outlays, and the public suffers correspondingly. Private companies are awarded profitable research contracts, which allow them first knowledge of whatever findings are uncovered. They can then initiate profit-making ventures after the uncertainties of development have been publicly financed.

Data compiled by two researchers for the period 1946–1962 on the number of patents assigned to business firms that have been major research contractors for the Atomic Energy Commission, the Department of Defense, and the National Aeronautics and Space Administration (the three agencies that accounted for nearly all the patents issued in this period under the government's special licensing policy to contractors) revealed that one-half of the patents acquired by contractors from their government-financed research and development were owned by twenty large corporations. Besides, twenty corporations performed two-thirds of the research and development undertaken by industry for the federal government. Remarkably, the researchers concluded, "we do not look upon the concentration of these patents as a serious matter."[9]

The National Aeronautics and Space Administration (NASA) has funneled billions of federal dollars to private contractors for space research. One result is Comsat, a corporation thoroughly committed to profit-seeking while the social informational needs of the domestic, to say nothing of the international, economy go begging.

To repeat, the prime feature of governmental expenditures on information is the buttressing of the private corporate sector to the detriment of the public sphere. This in turn provides the basis for the second distinctive characteristic of the government's information-producing role: its heavy direct and indirect support for the instrumentation, psychological and material, of coercion and persuasion.

The government has since World War II invested the major portion of its research and development funds—the largest component in its total informational budget—in those projects that directly support the most aggressive needs and impulses of the corporate economy. The capacity to wage global nuclear war in numerous ways, and the ability to intervene militarily almost instantly in any part of the world, are the main achievements resulting from the hundreds of billions of research-and-development dollars spent over the last quarter of a century.

One writer observes that, "The giant R&D [research and development] spenders are the Pentagon, NASA, the Atomic Energy Commission and the Department of Health, Education and Welfare."[10] Yet this remark gives the misleading impression that the nation's health and welfare share significantly, if not equally, in the distribution of national research expenditures. Table One is instructive on this point.

In 1970, over four-fifths of the national government's research and development expenditures were concentrated on war and war-related areas (defense, atomic energy, and space). This may, in fact, be an understatement of the degree to which the government is spending money on research for aggressive ends. Military expenditures may be concealed in the "civilian" budgets of the Commerce, Interior, and Agriculture Departments as well.

By contrast, Health, Education and Welfare research, though the fourth largest expenditure by a government department, amounted to eight per cent of the overall federal R&D budget in 1970, hardly adequate to encourage the belief that the real needs of the people are the dominant consideration in the government's research outlays.

Substituting man-years of effort on government research and

TABLE ONE

*FEDERAL EXPENDITURES ON RESEARCH AND DEVELOPMENT, 1970**

Department	*Millions of dollars*
Agriculture	288
Commerce	118
Defense	7424
Atomic Energy Commission	1346
NASA	3699
Health, Education & Welfare	1235
Interior	153
National Science Foundation	293
All other	542
Total	15,098

* U.S. Bureau of the Census, *Statistical Abstract of the United States, 1971* (Washington: U.S. Government Printing Office, 1971), p. 510.

development for dollar expenditures, another study confirms this conclusion:

. . . from 1961 to now [1972], the federal government supported (i) 2 million man-years of defense R&D, *(ii) about 1 million man-years of space* R&D, *and (iii) about 175,000 man-years of non-civilian nuclear* R&D. *In contrast, (i) the total of all housing, urban, social and crime research that the federal government* has *ever funded is less than 13,000 man-years; (ii) the total* R&D *sponsored by the federal government for nonaviation transportation is of the order of 10,000 man-years; (iii) since 1969, 53,000 man-years of* R&D *have been expended by the federal government for environmental improvement.*[11]

These R&D expenditure patterns, though they reveal the main thrust of the government's interest in information, hardly tell the whole story. Another federally financed informational operation, impossible to explore thoroughly for obvious reasons, is the intelligence activities of numerous government agencies. Intelligence, it should be remembered, is the military term for information. The chronicler of the United States intelligence establishment, Harry Howe Ransom, defines it this way: "The pursuit of intelligence is the pursuit of information required for decisions or action. The information gained—the product—is substantive intelligence."[12]

The intelligence operation has accompanied the expansion of the American corporate system in its global quest for profits. Collecting information about the "enemy" or the "potential enemy" is now a mammoth job in Imperial America. Naturally, the definition and identification of the enemy continually change to meet the shifting needs of a worldwide business system intent on holding and extending its international position.

Not even the home front can be taken for granted. Senator Sam Ervin's Senate Subcommittee on Constitutional Rights heard testimony in 1971 on the widespread surveillance of civilians by military intelligence. The Committee reported that "the monitoring was far more extensive than we had imagined. In all, the Army appears to have had over 350 separate record centers containing substantial files on civilian political activity." The report continues, ". . . one can guess that Army intelligence had reasonably current files on the political activities of at least 100,000 civilians unaffiliated with the armed forces . . . [Moreover] as of December 31, 1970, the Defense Central Index of Investigations alone reported 25 million index cards representing files on individuals and 760,000 cards representing files on organizations and incidents . . . the surveillance dates back not to the Newark and Detroit riots of 1967 but to the reestablishment of Army Counterintelligence on the eve of the Second World War."[13]

Numerous national governmental agencies handle investigations of one sort or another. Clearly, they include the FBI, the Treasury, and the Secret Service, and many other agencies are similarly engaged. Senator Ervin's subcommittee discovered that the Civil Service Commission "maintained since World War II an index file of 2,120,000 cards containing lead information relating to possible questions of suitability involving loyalty and subversive activity." There was, in addition, "an index of 10,250,000 cards on personnel investigations made by the Commission and other agencies since 1939 on applicants, employees and private contract personnel of industrial concerns."[14]

The diligent subcommittee also uncovered the existence of similar lists in other government agencies. Senator Ervin described the special information held by the Federal Communications Commission: ". . . they maintain a checklist which now has about 10,900 names. This checklist, in the form of a computer printout, is circulated to the various bureaus within the Commission. It contains the names and addresses of organizations and individuals whose qualifications are believed to require close examination in the event they apply for a license."[15]

It is extremely difficult to determine accurately the dollar resources expended on these informational activities, but they are considerable. Ransom wrote in 1970 that "direct expenditures by CIA between 1960 and 1967 probably amounted to between $500 and $750 millions of dollars annually."[16] This estimate seems low when compared with other accounts. Also, the CIA is just one, though perhaps the most important, of at least six federal agencies engaged in intelligence operations abroad. The cost of the Pentagon's worldwide intelligence-gathering activities, entirely separate from the CIA's, was estimated at $2.9 billion annually in 1970.[17] For all intelligence activities carried on by the United States Government, the annual cost is estimated at $5 billion; the number of people involved in these operations abroad is believed to be at least 200,000, of whom 150,000 are military.[18]

There is another cost to the nation, in addition to the skilled labor power and money expended to engage in these destructive informational activities. Intelligence operations are, by definition, clandestine and closed to public scrutiny. When a significant fraction of the government's expenditures supports intelligence-gathering, it is inevitable that the secrecy that surrounds this work begins to spread to other governmental activities. This is the situation today. Hearings before a congressional subcommittee in 1971 revealed that there are twenty million classified documents within the federal apparatus.[19] Furthermore, "The National Archives now has in its possession an estimated 160 million pages of classified documents dating from the start of World War II and over 300 million pages dating from 1946 to 1954."[20]

The cost of administering the government's security classification system for the four agencies which produce the bulk of the government's classified documents—the Department of State, the Atomic Energy Commission, the Department of Defense, and the National Aeronautics and Space Administration—is estimated at $126 million annually.[21]

Governmental informational activities, overt and covert, are intended to promote private economic and national military power. This power, in turn, enhances corporate profit-making capacity domestically and internationally. The annual cost of these informational operations is huge. Dollars are not spared when the communications interests of the vital national power centers are concerned; it is different when the informational needs of ordinary people are involved.

Though television has been recognized for years as the chief communications medium in America, the country is still waiting for the establishment of a securely supported, noncommercial national system of public television. Since its inception in the late 1940s, television has been, with unimportant exceptions, a commercial enterprise, serving essentially as a marketing instrument. Only in 1967 did efforts to develop a noncommercial national system have even limited success. Since then there has been an annual struggle over budgets. Meager funds have been appropriated, but never for longer than one year at a time, a condition that is crippling artistically and operationally but wonderfully effective as a means of program control. The effort to secure a two-year budget for fiscal 1973–1974, with provision for a very modest increase in funding ($65 million the first year and

$90 million the second) was vetoed by the President in 1972,[22] a near-emasculation of the system.[23]

Informational activities that are not directly supportive of the corporate–governmental complex, receive only limited assistance at best. Though public television, as presently constituted, offers little threat to the established order,[24] it is still viewed with suspicion by national power-wielders. The extent to which it is kept impoverished is evident in Table Two, a comparison of expenditures per citizen for TV in a few countries with fairly comparable levels of economic activity:

TABLE TWO

*ANNUAL EXPENDITURES PER CITIZEN FOR TV**

U.S.: commercial TV (total advertising revenue for networks and stations)	$13.96
Canada: CBC-TV (partly commercial)	7.16
Great Britain: BBC-TV (noncommercial)	3.29
Japan: NHK-TV (noncommercial)	2.90
United States: public TV	.74

* Douglas Cater, "The Politics of Public TV," *Columbia Journalism Review* (July/August 1972), p. 13.

Under the Nixon Administration, the condition of public television, hardly robust to begin with, has deteriorated alarmingly. Not content to withhold federal financial support, it has harassed into retirement the top officers of the Corporation for Public Broadcasting, and the few meaningful current-affairs programs are being eliminated. The newly appointed president of the Corporation, Henry Loomis, was formerly a director of *The Voice of America*, and most recently served as deputy director of the United States Information Agency. *Variety* viewed the Loomis appointment as an indication that "President Nixon has become executive producer of public television,"[25] and called the system "The Nixon Network."

The Dissemination of Information

The complement of information production and collection is information dissemination. The factors that influence and shape the production of information in the United States are equally observable in the process of information distribution. The dominant interests of the state–capitalist economy determine the character of, and controls on, the information flow. This is evident in three areas of information dissemination at the national governmental level: the government as propagandist in the international arena; as public relations agent at home; and, lastly but perhaps most significantly, as controller and manipulator of the vast informational supplies in its possession.

The Government as Propagandist

The establishment in 1953 of the United States Information Agency as the official governmental instrument for foreign communications coincided with the post-World War II increase in American enterprise and influence abroad. As American foreign policy assumed its task of thwarting or controlling social change in other nations to protect investment opportunities for American business ("preservation of the free world" is the customary euphemism for this objective), an official organ was deemed necessary to explain these policies to understandably perplexed locals. A Presidential Memorandum in 1963 made this quite explicit: The USIA, it said, should "help achieve United States objectives by . . . influencing public attitudes in other nations."[26]

Though there has been some official squeamishness about admitting the basic function of the USIA, it is difficult to obscure. Alan Wells writes, "It is often claimed by overseas nationals that

USIA is a propaganda organ of the United States government. That is precisely what it is set up to be, and as such it has been quite successful." Wells quotes a former director of the Agency: "I can report proudly that the exhibits, broadcasts, telecasts, films, books, pamphlets and periodicals produced by the U.S. Information Agency are now regarded as models by the professionals engaged in the *arts and crafts of persuasion*."[27]

To disseminate information and images about the United States and the rest of the world that accord with the perspectives and intentions of American power-wielders, the USIA employs over ten thousand people (a little less than half of them American citizens), spends an annual budget of almost $200 million (more than four times the federal appropriation for domestic public broadcasting), and engages in a comprehensive international media effort. Its radio arm, *The Voice of America*, broadcasts daily in thirty-five languages over five transmitting facilities in the United States. These are relayed abroad through numerous overseas stations, some of which are located in Morocco, Liberia, Thailand, Ceylon, Greece, West Germany, Okinawa, The Philippines, Rhodesia, South Vietnam, and England.[28]

In what must be a classic description of the work of any propagandist, a former director of the USIA's motion picture and television service described its radio service thus: "*The Voice of America* attempts only to put facts—that would otherwise seem negative to a foreign audience—in a context of truth."[29]

Books, films, telefilms, magazines, and periodicals are made available by the USIA to foreign media and foreign nationals. Though it is not supposed to be a clandestine organization, its operations are not always directly visible. Often materials distributed to the local media are used without attribution, making the message less identifiable and therefore seemingly more independent and genuine.[30]

The USIA has had more than its share of criticism, domestically as well as in the countries in which it operates. Its problems abroad are understandable. Attempting to sugarcoat policies that may be antithetical to the national interests of the countries in which it is active, the USIA is bound to be at the center of frequent conflicts. At home, the situation is more complex, and often more than a little ironic.

As most media specialists now thoroughly understand, effective political messages must be low-keyed and occasionally even mildly self-critical. USIA professionals who attempt to use this approach often find that the subtleties of their techniques of persuasion are lost on some of the domestic reactionaries who must approve their funding. They encounter, therefore, the annual trauma over appropriations. In these recurring confrontations, the most adept ideological salesmen of the American corporate economy are forced to be defensive about the quality of their efforts.

Every so often the holdings of the USIA's overseas libraries are scrutinized to insure the absence of informational material and literature critical of the goals and aims of official United States policy. In fact, the USIA is kept on a very short rein. Its director, a presidential appointee, is hardly likely to misinterpret the basic informational perspectives that domestic controllers wish to see transmitted internationally. In addition to the annual congressional review, the USIA's ongoing activities are monitored by the United States Advisory Commission on Information, a presidentially appointed panel which oversees, in a very general way, the USIA's work.

The Commission is staffed with the most reliable representatives of the corporate economy, generally individuals with considerable professional expertise in the media. Its present members include Dr. Frank Stanton, former president of the super-conglomerate CBS, who was chairman of the Commission from 1964 to 1971; Hobart Lewis, president and editor-in-chief of *Reader's Digest*, a magazine with a domestic circulation of 18,000,000 and eleven overseas editions; and George Gallup, the pollster who has had a continuing close relationship with the government.

Supplementing the USIA are less-publicized organs of political–cultural penetration, some of which have come into prominence in recent years. In 1971, Senator Clifford Case disclosed that the CIA had been financing *Radio Liberty* and *Radio Free Europe*, which broadcast respectively to Eastern Europe and the Soviet

Union, since 1951. The most remarkable aspect of this disclosure is that it took twenty years to be made. A communications complex that employs thousands of people and has received during its lifetime about $500 million in federal appropriations is scarcely an obscure operation.[31] The American mass media ignored this story for two decades, not because it was unnewsworthy but because of their accommodation to, and complicity with, the imperial objectives of American postwar expansion.[32]

Long after changing currents of international politics had made it necessary to disclose the connection of these broadcasting stations with the intelligence services, the Under-Secretary of State for Political Affairs continued to justify their operations (with new and openly acknowledged governmental financial support) on the grounds that they serve as "a free and independent press."[33] Congress voted overwhelmingly in 1972 to extend the life of both facilities for at least another year. The $38.5-million appropriation approved for continued broadcasting to Eastern Europe and the Soviet Union for the fiscal year 1972–1973 is not much less than the annual sum allocated by Congress to the domestic Corporation for Public Broadcasting.

Wherever significant social change has occurred or may occur around the world, American transmitters are busy disseminating doubt about the new social forms and glorifying the acquisitive–consumerist system. Erik Barnouw has estimated that the once-clandestine communications efforts of the United States Government cost $100 million annually.[34]

The Government as Public Relations Agent

Writing about government public relations, Hillier Krieghbaum, a recent president of the Association for Education in Journalism, reported that "the Associated Press in 1967 estimated that the U.S. executive branch of the government spent approximately $400,000,000 on public information; two years later, Profs. William L. Rivers and Wilbur Schramm of Stanford University said that 'federal expenditures on telling and showing the taxpayers cost more than double the news-gathering budgets of the two major American wire services, the three television networks and the ten largest U.S. daily newspapers."[35] In 1970, a United States Budget Bureau study set the PR bill for selected governmental agencies at $164 million.[36]

Whatever the amount, it is substantial. Should such outlays be cause for concern? Krieghbaum has this to say: "The public needs some of this information; for instance, the National Weather Service predicts sunshine, rain, or snow; the Census Bureau supplies the best statistics on how many of us there are, what we do, where we live, and much other material; and the Bureau of Labor Statistics releases figures on the cost of living . . . But part of it cannot escape classification as almost pure propaganda."[37]

The government has a legitimate reason to impart information to the public about its activities, and the public has a vital need to be informed about these matters. But, as is the case with governmental production and collection of information, its social utility is heavily dependent on the character and orientation of the governmental agencies involved. Put differently, who is undertaking the dissemination of information and what purposes are thereby served? In short, *is public awareness heightened or diminished by the information disseminated?* This is a crucial criterion for appraising any information distribution.

Awareness is an alerted state of consciousness, a sensitivity to reality that precedes action. Accordingly, if consciousness is dulled and awareness impaired, one's sense of danger diminishes and one's well-being can be threatened. Aroused consciousness—the ultimate strength of human existence—is perhaps the only reliable force which can lead to change in the material–institutional environment. If it is undermined, society is in a grave condition.

For this reason, the governmental agencies currently most deeply engaged in public relations should be a source of the greatest unease. As we have come to expect, the most important governmental press agent is the Pentagon. We have Senator J. William Fulbright to thank for making some of these hitherto-veiled operations public. Senator Fulbright's book, *The Pentagon Propaganda Machine*,[38] based on speeches he delivered before the

United States Senate late in 1969, is a revealing study of the mechanics of governmental information management.

Thirty years of war and preparations for war, costing more than a trillion dollars, have created a standing army of millions and military installations in every corner (and some centers) of the world, a presence which Fulbright calls "a part of our environment, like pollution." But the Senator is focusing on a very different sort of environmental destruction. Nothing less than the crippling of the national consciousness is his subject.

What has happened, in brief, is that a "monstrous bureaucracy" at the service of the nation's armed forces has extended itself into information processing. Though perhaps inevitable, after decades of dependence on military "solutions," the highly organized machinery for mind management is not just another facet of the now well-known military–industrial complex. It represents an alarming step toward human manipulation that dwarfs the relatively small-scale issues of contract lobbying and business–military payola.

Originally created for the commendable purpose of imparting information to the public about its activities, the communications structure of the Department of Defense has grown into an enormous public relations operation—"the largest advertising agency in the world"—employing thousands of publicists and ancillary image agents and spending tens of millions of the public's tax dollars to persuade the citizenry of the utility of its heavy financial contribution to military security.

In this self-serving enterprise, the American people are the targets of a varied assortment of military public-relations tactics. Pentagon-organized tours of American military installations for foreign and domestic journalists are a special favorite. Since American bases dot the globe, the satisfaction such junkets afford can be considerable. Community leaders, from college deans to Rotarians and savings-and-loan executives, are also recipients of the military's largesse. Each service, moreover, participates in the slippery business of mass persuasion. The Army, for instance, has kept its television crews busy filming acceptable footage of its Vietnamese activities, emphasizing whatever can be regarded as affirmative. These reels, incidentally, are widely shown on commercial television as "public affairs" programs. This neat trick relieves private broadcasters of the responsibility and cost of producing independent informational material and provides the military with invaluable access to the national viewing audience.

A Pentagon speakers' bureau makes admirals, generals, and, occasionally, enlisted men with proper credentials available for the asking to businessmen's clubs, women's groups, patriotic assemblies, and assorted municipal gatherings. The Navy opens its ships for public visitation in domestic ports of call. The armed forces' radio and television system, "the world's largest television and radio network under single control," with 204 radio and 80 television land-based stations and 56 radio and 11 television stations on Navy ships at sea, not only provides American servicemen with a carefully edited version of the world's daily events, but reaches into the homes of additional millions of people within range of its signals.

The military has still other instruments of persuasion at its disposal. Military facilities are offered to commercial film-makers who will portray the armed forces in a suitably uncritical fashion. The Army mustered troops and a huge depot of equipment, practically on lend-lease terms, for John Wayne's film "The Green Berets," which rhapsodized about the United States' role in Vietnam. The Navy, not to be outdone, offered its men and squadrons on an equally philanthropic basis to Darryl Zanuck when he shot "Tora! Tora! Tora!"—Hollywood's version of the Japanese attack on Pearl Harbor.

The press agentry of the government is not limited to the informational tricks performed by the Pentagon. The other major beneficiaries of large information-research budgets, the favored government departments of the Imperial Society, are also heavily engaged in winning further public support of their projects. The Atomic Energy Commission and the National Aeronautics and Space Administration are especially active.

It is difficult for the AEC to become too enthusiastic about its chief products—nuclear weapons. Prudence, if not ethics, demands that most of its PR concern itself with the life-supporting aspects of atomic research, such as they may be.

With NASA the situation is different. Though deeply involved with military and militarily related programs, it can stage what appears to be a good, nonideological spectacular—a moonshot—whenever there is the slightest indication that the general population's interest in space is flagging.

A study of NASA's public relations found that the astronauts were made to appear as "larger-than-life scientists–athletes, Buck Rogers, Jack Armstrong, and the Hardy Boys rolled into one," while they are really little more than "overglamorized pilots." Reflecting on this, one writer observed that ". . . the public got its heroes, reporters got good news copy, and NASA, at least in the early years, got massive federal funding."[39]

Unfortunately the outcome is not all harmless, if wasteful, popular circuses for the global audience of hundreds of millions. Under the guise of exploring the heavens, NASA has supplied the American imperial system with the instrumentation for global espionage, as well as the means for almost instantaneous military intervention. Its efforts, though hypothetically applicable to useful and desirable ends, have to date been directed largely to the military and commercial aggrandizement of the corporate economy it serves.

A congressional report on these matters observed: "It is axiomatic that the requirement for Government agencies to inform the public about their activities can result in propaganda. The line between 'public information,' 'publicity or public relations,' and 'propaganda' is fine indeed and, like beauty, is often in the eye of the beholder."[40]

When government foregoes its commitment to the well-being of all the people and administers mostly to the interests of the powerful, it is inevitable that its informational role will follow the same course. Information management replaces information, and popular understanding is further reduced.

The Government as Information Manager

The federal government has thus far been presented as a more-

or-less unified, though imperfectly functioning, structure that presides over the national administrative apparatus. It is now necessary to modify this image somewhat.

The government, no less than other major social institutions, has been affected by the forces that have pushed the country onto the imperial course it has taken for two-and-a-half decades. In the informational sector, this development has been obscured by governmental reorganizations and administrative shuffles, and by the growth and decay of bureaucratic agencies. All the same, one central development stands out. While the flow of governmentally produced or supported information grows larger and larger, *access to and control over the flow of communications has become more and more restricted within the government itself*, to say nothing of the exclusion of the public-at-large.

Could it be otherwise? The bureaucracy's corporate–military supports are enormously wealthy and influential, but its popular base is very narrow. In championing the interests of a tiny, though powerful, sector of society, the governing elite must find the dependability of the vast remaining sector increasingly worrisome. How to explain to the general public the real reasons for global military "incursions," mass civilian surveillance, or any of the other programs required to control a society in an advanced stage of crisis?

And thus we have the truly incredible situation of the Congress of the United States complaining about its lack of information. The chairman of the Subcommittee on Government Operations declared in 1972 that "in recent years there has been an accrual of power by the Presidency at the expense of the Congress, with the Congress increasingly unable to get certain kinds of information central to its legislative and constitutional responsibilities."[41]

Another congressman calls attention to the disproportion in power that affects information flow inside the government: "One of the problems in the Congress is that we have very inadequate staff, even on committees. We just have a handful of people. The Department of Defense, the President's Office, the executive agencies have literally thousands of people, the most up-to-date information available, the most up-to-date equipment available, and everything else at their disposal. And we are severely handicapped in obtaining essential information."[42]

Exclusion from information has become the most formidable instrument of control inside the government itself. This condition is most advanced in the Executive Branch. George Reedy, former press secretary to President Lyndon B. Johnson, has described the changes that have encouraged the shift of control over information to a new corps of bureaucrats outside the traditional agencies of government. These new power-wielders are concentrated in the White House, comprising the President's personal staff. The implications of this development for general access to information are thus noted by Reedy:

. . . you are beginning to get a tremendous amount of the actual operation of the Government centered in the White House itself where it is covered by executive privilege. I think from the standpoint of . . . access to information . . . one of the principal problems that has to be faced is the fact that new agencies are being created in the White House, agencies where information is gathered, collected, and used in a manner that formerly characterized agencies like the Defense Department, State Department, Labor Department, et cetera . . . Somewhere along the line, we have to take a very careful look at this fundamental problem of the new forms of organization that are arising, of the new White House staffs that are really no longer personal advisers to the President and who, from a realistic standpoint, should not be considered in that category, but who are housed within the White House confines and therefore fairly invulnerable to the press.

Reedy concludes:

What we are doing is transferring all of the staff levels, that is, all of the important staff and all of the important functioning of the Government into one new huge super-agency, that is relatively invulnerable to Congress and newspaper attack.[43]

How far this process has progressed is documented in a special report prepared by the Library of Congress' Congressional Research Service, and quoted by Representative William S. Moorhead in hearings before his Subcommittee on United States Government Information Policies and Practices. Moorhead observes:

In 1939 there were six advisers to the President, none listed under White House Staff or Executive Office Staff. By 1954 that had gone up to 25 advisers, 266 White House staff, 1,175 Executive Office staff, but by 1971 the original 6 advisers had jumped to 45, White House staff to 600, and the Executive Office staff to 5,395. This study also shows that it is not only the State Department affairs that are being handled in the White House, but also affairs of the Department of Commerce in which it is stated that the important man to see is not the Secretary of Commerce but a White House aide, Mr. Peter Flannigan.[44]

Representative Moorhead noted some of the consequences of this expansion in the White House staff:

. . . we are now witnessing a geometric expansion of the White House staff—with policymakers from the agencies and departments drawn in under the spurious White House umbrella of 'executive privilege' . . . since 1969 the White House staff has expanded by almost 100 percent. Amazingly enough, many of these persons are considered personal advisers to the President and will not appear before Congress.

Earlier this year [1972], *this subcommittee wanted Mr. Herbert Klein, the President's director of Communications, to appear with a panel of former press aides. He refused to appear.*

The subcommittee also invited Mr. David Young, primary drafter of the new Executive order on classification. He refused to appear. Even Donald Rumsfeld, head of the Cost of Living Council, refused to appear before this subcommittee, inappropriately, I think, donning his hat as an adviser to the President.

I ask the White House—what is the Congress supposed to do?

Are we to accept White House assertions that all is well and be content with the benign claptrap oozing from the basement of the White House as prepared by a former advertising 'flack' for Disneyland [Ron Ziegler, Presidential Press Secretary]? *I think not.*[45]

A particularly egregious example of this development is the Office of Telecommunications Policy (OTP), created in 1970 inside the White House. This agency advises the President on such communications issues as satellite communications, cable television, public broadcasting, and license renewal policy for commercial broadcasters—all matters ostensibly under the jurisdiction of the Federal Communications Commission.

Representative Lionel Van Deerlin inquired into this mushrooming operation and commented:

In less than two years, President Nixon's White House Office on Telecommunications has shown signs of becoming the newest Washington 'empire.' Its staff of experts is already five times the size of a congressional committee staff with similar jurisdiction. Serving this new executive think tank are 65 fulltime employees. That's more people than the White House employed for all purposes prior to World War II.[46]

Torbert H. MacDonald, chairman of the House Subcommittee on Communications, charged that the OTP had established an ancillary unit in the Department of Commerce, and that between the OTP and the Commerce group "more than 300 bodies and more than $10 million [are] doing work which the Congress assigned to the FCC nearly 40 years ago.[47]

The accession of Henry Kissinger as foreign policy advisor to the President has removed from congressional inquiry practically the entire area of foreign policy. Kissinger and his National Security Council staff, "which has usurped the field of American diplomatic affairs," refuse to testify before congressional committees —formerly a routine State Department obligation—claiming executive privilege.[48]

Some of the most crucial functions of government, and information pertaining to them, are being totally withdrawn from public and congressional scrutiny and sheltered in inaccessible enclaves under executive control. Under these new arrangements, even the forms of representative democracy are destroyed.

Other departments and branches of government, especially those that exercise real power over the economy, are no less eager to maintain as much secrecy as possible over their operations. For example, the Government Accounting Office (GAO), whose legal function is to monitor and audit all governmental programs and activities approved by Congress, complains that it is denied information and data about numerous programs under the control of the Department of Defense, the State Department, the Internal Revenue Service, and other powerful agencies.

The Comptroller General of the United States, who is the Director of the GAO, was compelled to write to the Secretary of the Department of Defense in the fall of 1971 as follows: "I believe you can appreciate the depth of my concern at what appears to be an increasing effort within the Department of Defense to restrict the General Accounting Office's capability to carry out its responsibilities to the Congress in the field of international matters."[49]

Congress itself, which now bitterly criticizes the executive branch's information blackout, has a notably poor record when it comes to openhandedness. In its annual survey of congressional committee secrecy, the *Congressional Quarterly* found that 36 percent of all committee hearings in 1971 were held in closed session. In 1972, 40 percent of all hearings were secret. Moreover, this statistic seriously understates the real degree of congressional secrecy. The key committees—those in which vital decisions on war, taxes, and resource allocation are made—have a much higher percentage of sessions that exclude the public. The House Appropriations Committee, for example held 92 percent of its 455 meetings in private in 1971. The House Ways and Means Committee held 62 percent of its meetings in private. In the Senate, the committees with a higher-than-average number of closed meetings included Aeronautical and Space Sciences (30 percent), Armed Services (79 percent), Finance (47 percent), Foreign Relations (43 percent), and Rules and Organization (68 percent). The Atomic Energy Committee, a Joint Congressional Committee, ordered 35 percent of its meetings closed.[50]

Paradoxically, these trends have accelerated since the passage of the Freedom of Information Act, which went into effect on July 4, 1967. This act, the culmination of more than a decade of effort by its proponents, was supposed to have ended excessive governmental secrecy. Unfortunately, its coverage is so restricted that the agencies and offices most prone to withhold information are practically exempted from its provisions. Though any citizen is supposed to have the right, under this law, to examine the records of any governmental agency he may be concerned with, the act allows several exceptions. The most important exceptions, from the perspective of this analysis, are those that apply to the bases of the national power structure.

Withholding of information is allowed under the Freedom of Information Act by nine specific exemptions, of which the following three decisively undermine any significant movement toward the liberation of information: "(1) specifically required by Executive order to be kept secret in the interest of the national defense or foreign policy; (2) trade secrets and commercial or financial information obtained from a person and privileged or confidential; (3) geological and geophysical information and data, including maps, concerning wells."[51]

These exceptions put the war machine, foreign policy decisions affecting the empire, corporate practices, and resource decision-making under the blanket of informational privilege. For example, *New York Times* senior editor James Reston complained that "official secrecy makes investigation of war profits exceedingly difficult. The new freedom of information law covers Government contracts in theory, but efforts by the *New York Times* and others to get at the details have been turned aside on the ground that other laws protect the privacy of these contracts."[52]

Or again, the International Division of the GAO reported these experiences:

We were unable to complete our work and report on this assignment within a reasonable time because of the time-consuming screening process exercised by the Departments of State and Defense before making records available for our examination. Our work was seriously hampered and delayed by the reluctance of the Departments to give us access to the documents, papers, and records which we considered pertinent to our review. In general, we were given access to only those documents, papers, and records which we were able to specifically identify and request, and then we were given access only after time-consuming screening at various levels within the Departments.[53]

These, it must be recalled, were the experiences of an authorized, highly trained *governmental* unit, attempting to secure meaningful information from other governmental agencies. Imagine the problems that an ordinary citizen would encounter in trying to elicit data from these sources, however forcefully he or she might invoke the Freedom of Information Act.

At first sight, the government's informational activities may seem confused and somewhat irrational. A system that spends tens of billions of dollars annually to secure data, and makes the most vital information available only to a privileged few, is hardly socially efficient, much less performing according to any approximation of the rules of democratic governance. Yet the contradiction is explainable. Simply put, the maintenance of a private corporate monopoly economy and an overseas empire necessitates the inverted informational distribution pyramid that now characterizes both governmental and nongovernmental communications in the United States.

Government Information as a Profitable Resource

For a variety of reasons, most of the mechanics of governmental information production and dissemination—printing, processing, and circulation—have remained outside commercial channels. This has been the result of no intentional slight to private enterprise. As long as these operations were unprofitable, the business system looked in another direction. Now that the information industry has grown to its present imposing size, and all the risks of the growth process have been borne by the public, a new situation obtains. Private efforts are being made to gain access to government information that may have commercial value, and to participate on a profit-making basis in the management, processing, and dissemination of the data that the government is willing to release.

With respect to the commercial utilization of information generated with governmental support, those corporations which originally received the federal research and development contracts are, as has already been noted, in the best position to take advantage of the new processes and know-how they developed.

The profit system also permits certain individuals to reap windfalls from the government's information storehouse. Numerous illustrious former office-holders have engaged in this mining operation. The mechanics of enriching oneself off of privileged governmental data are especially instructive. One writer who examined this activity wrote, ". . . the public should understand that these memoirs [of former high government officials] often do use classified information, and that former officials sometimes profit from the sale in book form of classified information about events, which, at the time they take place, are not shared with the press and the public. Thus, the classification system has been used to deprive the American people of information which is later sold to them by the officials they elected, or by appointees of those officials. Yet the information is denied to Americans when it might be pertinent to the opinions they hold and to the way they express those opinions at the ballot box."[54]

Lyndon Johnson, for example, "took 31 million papers from the White House, 5.5 million pages on microfilm, 500,000 photographs, 2,010,420 feet of film and 3,025 sound recordings. . . . the first volume of the former President's memoirs, reportedly based heavily on classified documents, was published in the fall of 1971."[55]

Daniel Ellsberg, the man who released the Pentagon Papers for publication *without charge*, committed a serious violation of the private entrepreneurial ethic.

Another curious but illustrative form of commercial exploitation of government information was uncovered by Representative Frank Horton, a member of the House subcommittee studying the United States Government's information policies. Horton reported:

Last year [1971], I learned from a constituent who was required to register with the Treasury Department as a gun collector under the Gun Control Act of 1968, that his name, and 140,000 other names of gun collectors and dealers were being sold indiscriminately. The computerized mailing lists, sold by the Treasury, were being used by commercial firms seeking to sell firearms to persons on the list, to political candidates seeking support for their legislative stands against gun control, and to anyone else who could produce $140.00, or one tenth of a cent per name, to buy the list.[56]

More systematic and far-reaching efforts are being made to move the government's massive informational activities onto a thoroughly commercial course, despite all the inequities in information distribution this will produce. These efforts are receiving the full support and encouragement of the present Administration. One private organization assisting the move to privatize governmental informational activity is the Information Industry Association (IIA), the trade association of profit-making companies in the information field. An account of the Association's third annual meeting in 1971 reveals the warm collaborative relationship that now exists between business and government in this area. A. N. Spence, the Public Printer of the United States, told the meeting: "As many of you know, we are presently operating under a new Federal Printing Program established by the Joint Committee on Printing. This program places the emphasis on contracting all government printing that is determined to be commercially procurable out to private industry."[57]

A second important figure in the government's informational activities gave an equally enthusiastic endorsement of business–governmental collaboration. *Publishers' Weekly* reported:

Similarly, William Knox, first president and one of the founders of IIA, who has "gone over to the other side," now that he heads the National Technical Information Service of the Department of Commerce, made it quite clear that he was committed to encouraging private participation in that new service's ambitious program for public dissemination of Commerce's giant information-producing bureaucracy.[58]

Consensus was achieved with the comment of Melvin Day, information director of NASA, who oversees one of the federal government's largest information programs. Day, also chairman of the National Science Foundation's Committee on Scientific and Technical Information, declared, "I am personally committed to bringing the private sector into our effort—and my bosses at the NSF know this."[59]

Now that it has achieved billion-dollar status, both in the equipment it uses and the material it produces, the governmental information industry, is being "opened up" to commercial enterprise, much like the natural resources formerly held by the federal government. Government information—a national resource created with public funds—is on the way to becoming another commodity, made available or withheld according to marketing principles and profit-making calculations.

This means that those with resources can buy what they want. The less affluent—that is, most Americans—will be totally outside the stream of information distribution. The criterion of profitability applied to the distribution of government information will be still another cruel blow to the American Dream. If, as one scholar puts it, "the root of participation is information,"[60] the combination of corporate monopoly, governmental secrecy, manipulation, and, finally, the distribution of information on an ability-to-pay basis, marks the end of participation for most American citizens.

CHAPTER THREE

The Knowledge Industry: The Military–Corporate Component

The Department of Defense is one of the world's largest educators, and should be one of the world's best.

CLARK M. CLIFFORD
Former Secretary of Defense
Address before the National
Security Industrial Association
Washington, D.C.
September 26, 1968

UNTIL RECENTLY, public education, though saturated with commercialism, had remained largely autonomous in terms of decision-making. Now powerful forces are at work that may effect far-reaching structural changes in the administration, financing, and control of the country's system of public schooling. These developments are outgrowths of major shifts in the national economy.

The character of an economy is revealed in the work people do and the goods and services they produce. From a historical point of view, most Americans have shifted from agriculture to industry, and from rural to city–suburban living, in a relatively short time.

Since World War II, a new shift has occurred. The work force has been growing much more rapidly in the service and informational areas than in the goods-producing sector. This was highlighted in a 1962 study by Professor Fritz Machlup, who found that in 1958 knowledge production accounted for almost 29 percent of the gross national product and that its growth rate was twice that of other goods and services.[1]

One can, of course, take exception to Machlup's definition of "knowledge," but the fact remains that informational activities of one kind or another, useful or not, are developing very rapidly. Machlup, now updating his study, is reported to believe that more than 50 percent of the work force, students included, are presently associated with the knowledge industries.[2]

Another perspective, which compares somewhat different components in the national economy but makes a related point, is offered by a former president of the National Education Association. George D. Fischer, now chairman of an Educational Facility Center, a permanent exposition of educational materials produced by American industry, observes that "the education industry is second only to the defense industry in size."[3]

In short, it is becoming clear that the expanding informational sector is taking on the characteristics of a major macro-system that interrelates in unique but predictable and approved ways with the rest of the economy.[4] Though the final forms that these interrelationships will assume are not yet clear, there are some discernible trends. The same social dynamics that have produced the present structure of this country are influencing the institutional shape of the future: the knowledge market is expanding greatly, and much of the expertise to exploit that market is firmly in the hands of private industry and the military establishment.

The quality of information that may be expected from an institutional structure dominated by business and the military will be considered elsewhere. This chapter is concerned with the more general consequences of harnessing the public educational system to the narrow interests and goals of private profit-seeking corporations and military training programs.

It may seem odd to regard the Pentagon as part of the educational–informational structure of the United States, but for more than a quarter of a century the armed forces have been training millions of young men and acquiring in the process a fund of knowledge about the mechanics of teaching. David Shoup, former Commandant of the United States Marine Corps, takes note of this:

We are now a nation of veterans. To the 14.9 million veterans of World War II, Korea added another 5.7 million five years later, and ever since, the large peace-time military establishment has been training and releasing draftees, enlistees, and short-term reservists by the hundreds of thousands each year. In 1968 the total living veterans of U.S. military service numbered over 23 million, or about 20 percent of the adult population. . . . For many veterans the military's efforts to train and indoctrinate them may well be the most impressive and influential experience they have ever had—especially so for the young and less educated.[5]

In 1968, Clark Clifford, then Secretary of Defense, observed: "The Department of Defense is one of the world's largest educators, and should be one of the world's best. We train military people in 1500 separate skills, and our schools for service children are in 28 countries around the globe."[6]

The military services, which have extended and protected the American empire for the last three decades, have been the recipient of enormous budgets voted by otherwise economy-minded congressmen. Their staggering resources have permitted the armed forces to become the most innovative and experimental sector of the society—with tragic consequences for those who find themselves in the way of the American juggernaut.

The information-processing that made possible the sophisticated techniques of ecocide used against the Vietnamese people were developed and introduced by a closely knit industrial–military consortium. Nowhere else in the economy are automatic data-processing techniques more elaborate or advanced. An indication of how relatively underdeveloped the other agencies of the national government are can be adduced by the fact that "when fiscal 1972 began, the Federal Government was utilizing 5,400 computers, and eighty-eight percent of them were accounted for by the Department of Defense."[7]

The air war against the Vietnamese was heavily dependent on this technology. For example, "of the eleven American Air Force bases in Vietnam, eight had computerized support functions by the fall of 1970. The pride of the 7th Air Force is a complex computer system called Seek Data II, designed to pre-plan Vietnam air strikes and airlifts."[8]

The military has succeeded in combining theory (research on information systems and technology) and practice (utilization of the data-processing capabilities developed for use against obstacles to American imperialism). In the process, the Pentagon has emerged as one of the world's central informational systems, integrating such diverse fields as personnel training, tactics and logistics of warfare, electronic surveillance and espionage, and global (as well as local) public relations. In a ninety-page roster of federal libraries compiled in 1970, sixty pages were devoted to a list of libraries serving the armed forces.[9]

In 1968 the Pentagon revealed its ambition to branch out far beyond its traditional military role. It stood ready, it announced, to undertake a variety of social services, including various phases of the educational process hitherto reserved for civilian authorities.* [10]

* Just how far the Pentagon has moved in this direction, with full Presidential approval, is documented in one startling account of its Domestic Action Program (DAP). Under this program, the Department of Defense (DOD) provides summer camps for poor kids. "As of 1970, the total number of DAP activities involved 5,000 military institutions in all 50 states. Over 75 percent of the children in the summer programs were from 'disadvantaged' families in poverty-stricken ghetto target areas. . . . According to DOD statistics, DAP took 225,000 'disadvantaged youths' out of the ghetto in 1969. The number increased to 775,000 in 1970 (a 300 per cent jump) and to 2,700,000 in 1971 (an increase of 347 per cent)." The authors of the report conclude: "DAP threatens the very basis of the distinction between the military and civilian sectors of American society. As the military gradually absorbs the functions of other executive departments, unnoticed by

At the same time, the business community, including educators-turned-businessmen, was taking giant steps to dominate the market for educational materials while assuring the nation that the efforts of their mushrooming "learning corporations" are motivated, if not entirely by altruism, then at least by a quest for profits tempered with social concern.

Not everyone is enchanted with these developments. Fred Heddinger, who has been president of both the Pennsylvania School Boards Association and Pennsylvania Electronics Technology, Inc., made this assessment:

With the advent of new-found Federal funds to support education have come friends who want to share in this affluence of education at the Federal level. Big business, which could have directed its efforts toward educational goals long ago if it so chose, suddenly has realized that large new product and profit opportunities will exist if Federal educational agencies are wooed. . . . Former President Eisenhower, shortly before leaving office, issued a stern warning regarding the potential danger that exists from the powerful alliance of strongly funded military agencies and industries seeking such funds. . . . If this warning was justifiable in defense circles—and it was and is—it is even more applicable to education.[11]

Phi Delta Kappan, an important educational journal, devoted an entire issue to "The Military and Education." It warned that "there is little doubt about the growing power of the Pentagon and the willingness of Defense Department leaders to exercise that power in areas outside of its traditional functions." In its view, the problems arising from the "increasing intimacy of the

---

the public, the specter of an American society even more responsive to militarily defined priorities becomes frighteningly immediate." George D. Corey and Richard A. Cohen, "Domestic Pacification," *Transaction-Society* 9 (July/August, 1972): 17–23.

Note also the appointment of Elliot Richardson, former Secretary of the Department of Health, Education and Welfare, as Secretary of the Department of Defense.

military and civilian educational efforts . . . range from baffling to frightening."[12]

The military–industrial coalition's vision of a new empire in education is encouraged by government officials like Samuel Halperin, Assistant Secretary of Health, Education and Welfare, who announced in 1968: "Education is the growth industry of America . . . already, almost a third of our population is enrolled in one kind of school or another . . . Teachers, supervisors, administrators, and other educational personnel, now more than three million strong, will soon surpass the number of farmers . . . expenditures for education will rise . . . from $50 billion today to a projected $66 billion in 1975 (in 1965–66 dollars). In short, the impressive growth prospects of American education are worthy of your most serious attention."[13]

Though these "growth prospects" are somewhat less lustrous five years later, the pressure to bring education under the capacious government–business umbrella remains strong. And by any standard, education is no longer a fringe activity in the goods economy.

The convergence of several independent forces is likely to move the classroom onto the industrial production line: (1) The costs of maintaining the American Empire, against increasing worldwide resistance, continue to grow; (2) taxes to support the educational system, even at its present level, are unpopular; and (3) research on educational technology is accumulating. These trends, processed through the decision-making apparatus of a private profit-seeking economy, will result inevitably in the "need to economize" on education. When this decision is in fact made, if it hasn't been already, the barely visible movement to computerized learning in the schools can only accelerate.

Supplying schools and homes with the materials and hardware for the future instrumentation of learning is too tempting a prospect for business to leave in the hands of civil servants and local school administrators. It is no surprise that, in the absence of strongly supported national guidelines for public action, private firms are adopting new economic practices designed to capture a fresh source of profits in the already substantial education market. They are scrambling for shares in an open-ended, still poorly defined, but potentially rich knowledge industry. The immediate consequence is that education, which until recently was insulated against direct commercial intrusion, is now being surveyed as a potential enclave for massive profit-making.

A dramatic example of the "gold rush" to the new Klondike of education is the sweeping reorganization of the publishing industry. Producers of "software" learning materials have been absorbed by a clutch of electronics corporations, some of which have already begun the manufacture of educational hardware, the so-called learning machines.

The financial pages provide frequent evidence of the hurried tempo now characteristic of what was once the gentlemanly—and almost quiescent—publishing industry. Companies that produce the materials of learning—books, magazines, audio-visual aids, and the like—have been merging at a breathless pace and in a bewildering variety of combinations. While many of these combinations are of the traditional sort—one publisher acquiring another—the striking new feature of this phenomenon has been interindustry mergers.

The desire to produce or otherwise control educational material that may eventually be electronically programmed, and to extend their influence to all levels of the educational market, have led producers of hardware learning equipment, electronics firms, and mass media companies to move rapidly into the software fields. Thus, Radio Corporation of America (RCA) acquired Random House. International Telephone and Telegraph bought out Howard W. Sams & Company, a textbook and technical book publisher. The Columbia Broadcasting System took over Holt, Rinehart and Winston, a trade and textbook publisher, for which it paid $280 million, the highest price ever offered for a publishing company. International Business Machines merged with Science Research Associates, which in turn bought out Howard Chandler Company, a college text publisher in San Francisco.

The list goes on and on. Litton Industries, the industrial conglomerate, absorbed the American Book Company. Raytheon Company, an electronics corporation, acquired D. C. Heath, a textbook firm. Xerox bought University Microfilm, American Educational Publications ("My Weekly Reader"), Learning Materials, Incorporated, and R. R. Bowker, the publisher of the leading trade magazines, *Publishers' Weekly* and *Library Journal.* Ginn, one of the two largest elementary school textbook companies, was also taken over by Xerox. Time, Incorporated, together with General Electric Company, created the General Learning Corporation; along the way, Time acquired Little, Brown & Company, the venerable Boston book publisher. Sylvania Electric Products, a subsidiary of the General Telephone and Electronics Corporation, allied with *Reader's Digest* to investigate the potential of electronic systems in education. Harcourt, Brace Jovanovich, a major book publisher, joined with RCA to explore the learning process. The list of such acquisitions, consolidations, and mergers grows yearly.

The Authors League of America, in 1973, wrote to the Senate Subcommittee on Antitrust and Monopoly Legislation, to call its attention to "a massive wave of acquisition" in the publishing industry. It regarded this movement as a serious threat to the survival of an independent book publishing industry.[14]

It is not only the prospect of capturing the classroom that is motivating many of these mergers. Informal, para-educational activities are growing even more rapidly than institutionalized education, and are also prime targets for commercial penetration. Not by chance does *Fortune*'s 1972 compilation of the five hundred largest manufacturing corporations in the United States include *for the first time* companies in the motion picture and broadcasting industries. As the editor explains this new departure: "Even though, like publishing companies, CBS, ABC, MCA and Columbia Pictures Industries 'make' information and entertainment, they were excluded in the past because they are not manufacturing and/or mining companies as defined in the U.S. Office of Management and Budget's Standard Industrial–Classification Manual. The SIC definition remains our basic reference point for the industrial list, but making this one exception seems to us to provide a better-rounded description of the 500 (largest) universe."[15] Well might these information combines be regarded as manufacturers. Warner Communications Incorporated, a new name for an old conglomerate (McKinney Services, Incorporated), describes its range of interests thus:

Warner Communications Inc. is every facet of communications, including its newest manifestation, Cable Television. Warner Communications, Inc. is records and music publishing . . . is outstanding motion pictures for over half a century. . . .

We're publishing and distribution, with books and magazines for every taste. We're every imaginable form of TV, *from cartoon program to family comedies to original drama series to movies-for-television. By the word on the page or the image on the screen or the sound in the air—by whatever fantasy-come-true in the technological tomorrow, we will be there when the future happens.*[16]

This is not just puffery. Warner Communications Incorporated also has a hefty minority interest in the new feminist magazine *Ms.*

The tie-in of big business with Hollywood, evident from the earliest days of film-making, has broadened into numerous single-package ventures. The editor of *Variety*, summing up the show-business scene in 1971, reported: "Advertising agencies and industrial combines were getting into filmmaking in 1971. Witness Wells, Rich, Greene Agency cofinancing with Warner 'Dirty Little Billy,' or Quaker Oats bankrolling David Wolper's 'Willy Wonka and the Chocolate Factory,' or Xerox readying to produce 'family' film features. Book publisher Doubleday & Company is also going into film production. Mattel Toys . . . is backing producer Robert Radnitz in a series of eight features, one of which . . . is complete."[17] The Warner Communications conglomerate in 1972 had three of the nation's top ten box-office hits: "A Clockwork Orange," "Dirty Harry," and "What's Up, Doc?"

The phenomenon of business concerns depending on government contracts for much of their growth and profits, and exercising a powerful influence on national decision-making, has been a feature of American life since World War II. Now a new complex is emerging in the educational field, also reliant on government funds, though not necessarily exclusively, to sell its output. The educational–commercial combine, which I call "EDCOM," looks to the United States Office of Education (OE) for security and understanding. Much as the older, more experienced defense contractors have found a true friend in the Department of Defense, so too has the Office of Education forged bonds with the military establishment—the Pentagon and its industrial suppliers. The hazards of such an alliance are obvious.

The federal outlay for education—direct support to schools, colleges, and students—now exceeds $7 billion annually. Other education-related expenditures add an additional $8½ billion, bringing the total federal expenditure on education to almost $16 billion.[18] Though the educational boom in the seventies is not nearly as robust to date as it promised to be in the late sixties, education is still, despite temporary "hard times," a growth industry.

The education "business" remains, however, in the words of McGraw-Hill executive vice-president Robert W. Locke, "small potatoes": about $1.5 billion a year.[19] Still this is enough to warrant hopes for rewarding future payoffs, some of which are already visible. For example, The Learning Corporation of America, a subsidiary of Columbia Pictures Industries, Incorporated (not to be confused with *Time*–GE's General Learning Corporation), issued an *Urgent Announcement* in August, 1971, calling school administrators' attention to the early passage of the 1972 Education Appropriations bill, totaling $5,024,007,000. The company explained the sections of the bill that made funds available for the purchase of audio-visual materials—which it modestly offered to supply. Since most educational expenditures are still financed out of local and state revenues, the knowledge industry cannot rely on the Office of Education as the exclusive spigot for its money flow, but policies and plans established by the OE are expected to be influential guidelines for the 26,000 local school board purchasers of teaching materials.

School authorities who might provide American education with alternatives to the EDCOM approach are already excluded from the decision-making process. Testifying before a congressional committee, John Henry Martin, then superintendent of schools in Mount Vernon, New York, observed, "Big business has decided that the knowledge industry will be profitable [and] the center of gravity for educational change is moving from the old seats of power, the teachers' colleges, and the superintendent's office to the executive suite."[20]

The key positions in the EDCOM complex are already occupied. Business controls most of the production centers and the technology. The site of educational policy-making has shifted in recent years to the Office of Education in Washington, which appears to have been thoroughly infiltrated by representatives of the learning industry's technostructures. As J. Myron Atkin, dean of the University of Illinois' College of Education, wrote in 1967 in *The Educational Forum*, ". . . In fact, if one is inclined toward a conspiratorial view, it is possible to elaborate a detailed case for collusion between Federal officials and the emerging education industry. The intrigue is direct, if not necessarily overt; it may consist primarily of a free exchange of personnel between industry and the Federal Government . . ."[21]

Harold Howe, formerly United States Commissioner of Education, cited with pride the growing functional intimacy of business and education, reflected in the nature of the personnel and advisors of the OE. "At the Office of Education alone," he wrote in *Educational Technology* in 1967, "we have in the neighborhood of twenty business officials serving on our advisory committees—from electronics companies, from the Chamber of Commerce, from the television industry, from banking and a variety of other fields."[22]

Moreover, OE staff members are following the manpower migration pattern which has long been characteristic of the war-related government agencies and their private corporate suppliers. Though shifts are constant, and any list is out-of-date almost as soon as it is compiled, there have been some notable moves in recent years. Francis Keppel, the former United States Commissioner of Education, and his aide Francis Ianni joined *Time*–GE's subsidiary, General Learning Corporation; John Naisbitt, another former top Keppel aide, became assistant to the president of Science Research Associates, an affiliate of IBM. Robert Hills, a former Health, Education and Welfare official, became a director of government programs for Basic Systems, Incorporated, a subsidiary of Xerox. Edward L. Katzenbach, Jr., a former deputy assistant Secretary of Defense for Education, assumed the general managership of Raytheon Company's education division. An example of in-migration is Richard Louis Bright, who succeeded Ianni as director of the Office of Education's Bureau of Research: Bright was previously Westinghouse Corporation's director of instructional technology.

The vast apparatus of training and instrumentation that the Defense Department has operated since World War II, financed far more generously than is the grudgingly tax-supported public school system, has provided the Pentagon with a great deal of information about the learning process. For instance, "at Fort Ord, where 16,000 men train at a time, and at 10 other basic training centers across the country, watching television has become part of the new soldier's daily routine . . . The (United States Continental Army) Command currently owns a library containing hundreds of videotaped 'how-to-do-it' films that instruct the recruits on everything from how to salute to how to pull a grenade pin or repair an axle on an armored troop carrier. More than 4.8 million viewers watch the 'network' annually, making the Command the operator of the largest and most sophisticated closed-circuit television system in the world."[23]

The OE, on attaining a state of relative affluence, has found it natural to look to the experience of its governmental neighbor. Accordingly, Defense Department administrative and organizational techniques have been viewed by the OE with awe and respect, regardless of their appropriateness or relevance to what should be their entirely different objectives.

The business–military outlook of the OE is warmly encouraged by the defense and business communities. Close ties have been formed between the OE and the National Security Industrial Association (NSIA), which is the organizational epitome of the military–industrial complex.

In June, 1966, the Department of Defense, the Office of Education, the Department of Labor, and the National Security Industrial Association co-sponsored a Conference on Engineering Systems for Education and Training. At the meeting, some seven hundred representatives of military agencies and industrial organizations discussed educational technology and its future role in education and training. The stated purposes of the conference were:

To brief industry on the magnitude and kinds of Office of Education and Department of Defense education, training, and related support activities and the procedures for formulating policy related to these specific areas.

To inform industry on Defense Department and OE major problems and priority areas and to advise industry of possible solutions to education and training problems.

To give industry an idea about what areas they might explore in terms of future market potentials in the four billion dollar-a-year [Defense] *education and training program and in areas supported by OE.*

To develop rapport between industry and Defense and OE in seeking solutions to education and training problems.

Since this early effort at cooperation, more formal arrangements have been developed. Project Aristotle, an acronym for Annual Review and Information Symposium on the Technology of Training, Learning, and Education, has come into existence. This is "a volunteer organization founded at the suggestion of the Department of Defense under the administration of the National Security Industrial Association." The objective of Project Aristotle, according to its own brochure, "is to provide a structure to encourage continuing communications within the Government–Education–Industry community and to contribute to the advancement of quality and efficiency of the nation's education and training. This is being accomplished through ten co-operative task groups formed from over 250 volunteers—members of industry, government, national associations, and the educational community."[24]

As well as cultivating its military associations, the Office of Education has enthusiastically supported the prevailing Washington philosophy of turning over to private enterprise activities that have hitherto belonged to the governmental or nonprofit sectors of the society.

Fred Heddinger, the Pennsylvania School Boards Association's president, wrote in 1967 in the *Phi Delta Kappan* that, "prior to the passage of the Elementary and Secondary Education Act of 1965, the Office of Education had adhered to a policy of contracting with universities, colleges, and other non-profit institutions for research on education. Shortly after the passage of this bill, however, the Office announced that it now had the prerogative of contracting with industrial concerns and other profit-making organizations for such research and development."[25]

In addition, the OE supported an amendment to the law in 1966 that made more explicit its authority to move further in industry's direction. The ultimate step, however, toward enlisting the profit motive directly in the educational process was the development of so-called performance contracting—the application of business–military–government procedures to education.

Begun in 1969, these contracts between private firms and public schools or districts stipulate that the company will be paid according to how much children learn from the company's program, as measured by standard tests at the end of a given period. Programmed instruction is relied on heavily because the results are "measurable." Inevitably, learning is viewed as a mechanical operation. As one account put it: "Learning of (certain kinds) can be divided into discrete units; units can be labeled (with objectives) and tested. Students must acquire learnings—as many as possible. The system succeeds when the child tests 100 per cent. Learnings are things; since contractors are paid for student learning, learning, by implication, is a commodity to be bought and sold. Most performance contracting so far has tied simple, perhaps ill-conceived goals to crudely designed monetary rewards for the contractor."[26]

In performance contracting, all the dominant trends and objectives of advanced corporate capitalism come together. Training techniques developed by the war machine are applied for profit by firms that are themselves producers of, or contractors for, the new educational hardware. Everyone benefits but the subjects. The children of the most disadvantaged sectors of society, the racial minorities and the poor, are paraded through educational charades that promise to overcome rapidly their long-standing environmental deprivations.

Gary, Indiana, for example, with its predominantly black population, was an early laboratory for performance contracting. So too was Texarkana, on the Arkansas–Texas border. These "experiments" were heralded with the press agentry we have come to expect in a media-manipulated culture. Two years later, reappraisals seem in order.

In early 1972, the *Los Angeles Times* ran a front-page banner headline announcing, "Special Ghetto Classes Fail." The story read, "Reporting on a massive experiment the government said thousands of disadvantaged children who were failing in traditional classrooms performed no better when exposed to the teaching machines and educational psychology and other know-how developed by profit-making educational firms."[27] Despite these disappointing results, the system of privately contracted education is being extended to other urban areas where deprivation prevails. The Los Angeles Board of Education, for example, voted in mid-1972 to seek state funds for performance contracting.[28]

It is clear that the "educational" sector of corporate capitalism is not about to solve the deepening crisis in American schooling. But who could have imagined that to be its intent in the first place? More to the point, the education business has not abandoned its profit expectations of this "market." In fact, EDCOM is reaching out into the international field, where there are hundreds of millions of educationally "disadvantaged." *Publishers' Weekly* reports on a meeting in Paris in 1971, assisted but regarded as "unofficial" by UNESCO, in which "representatives of producers and distributors of educational materials in the major publishing countries . . . set the stage for a coordinated effort to meet the needs of developing countries. Initiated by its American participants, the U.S. delegation included representatives from Raytheon, *Time*, Inc., Grolier, and the McGraw-Hill Book Co."[29]

Since the beginning of the republic, education has been a public responsibility, regardless of the nation's meager resources in its early years. Now, ironically, at a time of overwhelming national affluence, it is in danger of being turned over to the exploitation of private profit-seeking organizations and the influence of the military.

EDCOM is a joint effort of business and the military to guarantee control of the kind of *trained* work force they require. At the same time, it provides a widening market for the teaching machinery, films, books, and other materials the combine produces. These arrangements will eventually affect millions directly and personally, children as well as adults.

The uncontrolled expansion of industrial monoliths in the educational–informational–cultural sector is a clear and present danger. No claims of industrial efficiency can reasonably outweigh the potential risk to the nation of cultural combines that sift the knowledge that passes through their privately administered conduits to organize learning systems that place a high premium on training but show slight regard for the educational development and true needs of the individual.

The emergence of gigantic, integrated informational complexes closely associated with a vast military structure poses a new threat to American society. These private informational–educational oligopolies are assuming the prerogative of processing the nation's culture according to their own parochial notions of efficiency and skill. At the same time, these super-corporations reveal less and less about their own inner workings. A Federal Trade Commission study published in late 1972 reported that the proliferation of conglomerates causes an "information loss." Information about the formerly independent companies that are taken over by the umbrella company "disappeared into the mass of the conglomerate."[30]

A military description of the utilization of educational technology is perhaps a fitting conclusion to this discussion. What follows is a metaphor developed by a West Point educational technologist before an International Communications Symposium in 1972:

> . . . *Let's consider a crude analogy. If we consider the classroom instructor as the "academic infantry," then why not organize the support capability as "academic artillery" with the academic equivalent of artillery forward observers, the academic equivalent of a fire support coordination center, and so on. Just as the organization of the artillery can encompass such diverse weapons as mortars, howitzers, guns, rockets, and guided missiles, why should not an academic support organization include such diverse educational technology weapons* [sic] *as viewgraphs, slides, filmstrips, motion pictures, television and computer-assisted-instruction? Forward observers become media consultants who work with individual academic departments, course directors and instructors to help them plan what kinds of media to use, when to use media, and when not to use media. A fire-support coordination center becomes central location for coordination of all media requirements and capabilities to assure that television is not used where single-concept films would be more appropriate and effective, or to assure that a slide presentation is not used when overhead projection transparencies would be better.*[31]

CHAPTER FOUR

Recreation and Entertainment: Reinforcement for the Status Quo

> *. . . the fabric of popular culture that relates the elements of existence to one another and shapes the common consciousness of what is, what is important, what is right and what is related to what else is now largely a manufactured product.*
>
> GEORGE GERBNER
> *Scientific American*
> September 1972, p. 154

IN THE UNITED STATES, where rising productivity permits the work force more and more released time, recreation and entertainment are growth industries with an enormous, though totally unacknowledged, cultural impact. In fact, there seems to be a widespread insistence that they have no impact at all. The explanation for this astounding denial requires analysis.

Though all the myths on which mind management depends are found in the recreational–entertainment products of the Madison Avenue–Hollywood word-and-image factories, one central myth dominates the world of fabricated fantasy; the idea that entertainment and recreation are value-free, have no point of view, and exist outside, so to speak, the social process.

An enormously diverse consciousness-processing apparatus,

utilizing all the familiar forms of popular culture—comic books, animated cartoons, movies, TV and radio shows, sports events, newspapers and magazines—takes full advantage of this totally false conception. The communications industry pumps out value-laden recreation and entertainment, denying all the while any impact beyond momentary escapism and a happy state of relaxation.

There is, as a particularly egregious example, the distinction between television and *educational* television, more recently called public television. According to this preposterous dichotomy, stoutly maintained by the recreationists, nothing that educates is transmitted on the heavily viewed commercial channels, news programs and documentaries aside. The notion that entertainment is not instructive must be classed as one of the biggest deceptions in history. Erik Barnouw, chronicler of American broadcasting, puts it this way: "To me entertainment is a poisonous concept. The idea of entertainment is that it has nothing to do with the serious problems of the world but that it fills up an idle hour. Actually, there is an ideology implicit in every kind of fictional story. Fiction may be far more important than non-fiction in forming people's opinions."[1] This observation, of course, is not limited to TV.

The process by which the products and imagery of the entertainment industry are absorbed into human belief structures is not easy to map. Precisely how an individual is affected by what he reads or sees or hears defies easy explanation. For our purposes, it is sufficient to identify the ideology of the corporate economy that saturates "pure" entertainment in America. It can be demonstrated that the content and form of recreational messages, far from being value-free, are deliberately designed to promote dominant institutional outlooks and behavior. "Popular entertainment," as Erik Barnouw says, "is basically propaganda for the status quo."[2]

This chapter examines three important and representative cultural–informational institutions that present themselves as totally nonideological: TV *Guide*, *The National Geographic*, and Walt Disney Productions, Incorporated, the enterprise responsible for the wide variety of Disney products. For reasons of accessibility and availability, published materials, rather than films, have been chosen for this analysis. A study of TV, radio, or film products would reveal, I am convinced, a similar, if not identical, pattern. For, despite Marshall McLuhan's insistence on each medium's uniqueness, there is an underlying similarity in the message flow with respect to basic systemic values. It is not, as McLuhan claims, that the "medium is the message," but that *all the media transmit the same message*, each in its own form and style. An exploration magazine's impact on readership cannot be measured against a televised professional football game's audience arousal. Their formats and the reactions they generate are worlds apart. What can be noted and compared, however, are the social messages interspersed in each. Does the pro game's intermission feature an Air Force fly-over, permitting thirty million viewers to participate vicariously in a military celebration masquerading as an entertainment? Does the exploration magazine run feature articles about the United States Navy as a "force for peace,"[3] introducing its considerable readership to the benign and salutary effects of the Navy's maneuvers?

These are the relationships, however difficult to gauge in terms of audience effect or to compare across the media, that are significant. The cumulative impact on the message-consumer of all the related stimuli in all the media is what has to be measured and appraised.

TV *Guide*—"Neutral" Information

It was inevitable that there would be a TV guide. Television, the 1970 census informs us, is more prevalent in American homes than bathrooms or telephones. 95.5 percent of the 67.7 million housing units had a TV set in 1970, and almost 30 percent had two or more sets.[4]

TV *Guide*'s primary task, after making a profit, is systematically to inform this vast audience of the week's offerings on the locally available TV channels. On the face of it, this is a straightforward informational service, an activity that could hardly be described as manipulative—until the functions of commercial television and the objectives of most commercial publishing in the United States are considered.

Commercial television, it will be recalled, is organized—and that term is appropriate—to deliver mass audiences to advertisers. The programming is the "filler" between the sponsors' messages. As *Variety*'s TV editor sees it: "The viewer is not the customer but only the consumer of television. He is what the advertiser buys like herds of cattle—$2.50 per thousand bulk, $4 to $8 per thousand select (young men, young women, teen-agers, depending on the product marketed)."[5]

Commercial publishing is yet another vehicle to round up audiences for sponsored products. In the case of TV *Guide*, the market functions of commercial TV and commercial publishing are combined handsomely. The magazine helps herd the national audience into the TV viewing pens, and in the process stampedes them through dozens of pages of advertising copy. (A note to skeptics: a full-page newspaper blurb announced the good news: "With its December 9th [1972] issue, TV *Guide* becomes the fourth magazine in publishing history to carry more than $100 million in annual advertising revenue.")[6]

The exposure to, and promotion of, consumer messages that TV *Guide* provides its advertisers is therefore two-dimensional. It is a primary transmission channel in its own right, and it serves also as a pied piper cajoling its massive readership to tune in, stay up, and buy what it sees pictured in black-and-white or living color.

Each week more than 17½ million copies of TV *Guide* are sold across the nation. The magazine, in keeping with its consumer emphasis, "is on sale in display racks at about 350,000 checkout counters in food outlets throughout the United States and Canada. All of the major food chains and many independent markets distribute it . . ." As one friendly observer unwittingly put it: "It is easy for the housewife to pick up a fifteen cent copy and shove it along with the cans and packages for tally at the cash register. TV *Guide* is as much a household staple as salt or cereal."[7] *Reader's Digest*, with a slightly larger circulation, is a monthly. TV *Guide*, on the basis of its weekly publication, is probably "the country's most characteristic [widely-read] magazine."[8]

As a convenience to television viewers, TV *Guide* performs a service which most Americans find not only harmless and unobjectionable—"it doesn't hurt anybody, and it pleases millions"[9] —but even helpful. It informs the public of what is currently available. But by accepting commercial TV as a healthy and deserving institution, and by adapting its own informational service to commercial TV's enhancement, TV *Guide* becomes an accessory to an enormous misrepresentation. The service it proffers is applied toward mind management and is thus an additional instrument for enslaving consciousness. Its own profit-seeking imperatives make this inevitable. It too is an adjunct of the corporate economy and fattens on the same diet of consumerism.

TV *Guide* is more of a moneymaker than most widely circulated commercial publications by virtue of its ties to another medium. As is the case with all profit-seeking magazines, revenues are derived mainly from advertising. The amount and quality of advertising, in turn, are a function of circulation (sales). TV *Guide* builds its vast circulation with the assistance of *free* TV advertising. "TV stations, in return for program advertising that TV *Guide* prints for them, give the magazine free commercial time."[10]

With this built-in advantage, TV *Guide* becomes a gold mine. A less obvious consequence of this arrangement is that the publication becomes utterly dependent on the continued well-being of the commercial television industry for its own survival and profitability. Any development that commercial television owners perceive as a threat to their balance sheets, TV *Guide* must perforce recognize as a threat to its own treasury—not because it is corrupt, but because its own circulation is contingent on the goodwill and solvency of the broadcasters.

Further strengthening the bonds between the magazine and the corporate economy are the advertising revenues it receives from those companies that use its pages. These are the familiar big producers of consumer goods—automobile and oil companies; food, liquor, and beverage concerns; household goods corporations; and, not surprisingly, the manufacturers of products denied access to television: cigarettes, as of 1971, and female "hygienic aids" until 1972.

Beholden to the corporate economy for its advertising revenues and free publicity, TV *Guide* repays its benefactors in full, as a marketing tool and as a "neutral" informational source which is, in reality, partisan to the hilt.

TV *Guide* replicates the form and content of the medium it reviews weekly with so much admiration and so little critical judgment. Commercial TV's standard package of variety shows, personalities and celebrities, sports, and chitchat, with occasional forays into "serious issues," is reproduced every seven days. Small talk about the medium is spicily retailed, and "timely" articles on "whither the FCC" appear sufficiently frequently to create a (mistaken) impression of public responsibility. The magazine trys to sustain interest in TV as it is, encouraging people to accept what exists as the best that could possibly be hoped for. The TV quizzes, gossip, and crossword puzzles focus attention on what is already on the air. TV *Guide*'s preoccupation with these absolutely irrelevant offerings makes them appear reasonable and eminently worth viewing. TV *Guide*, in short, legitimizes what should be challenged while claiming only to be providing information.

The appearance of neutrality completely vanishes when TV *Guide*'s editorial content is examined; yet its departure from objectivity probably goes all but unnoticed by most of its huge readership (skimmership?). Conditioned by *the entire media system* to avoid concentration, most purchasers are not too likely to read the brightly assembled, short, and easily understandable "thought" pieces on satellite television, cable TV, the FCC, European programming, or the future of cassettes. In any event, the main message of the magazine—the endorsement of commercial television as it is presently constituted—can hardly be missed, even without reading the "heavy" pieces. This message is received automatically merely by picking up the magazine and scanning its contents. It is evident in the headlines, advertisements, pictures, colors, broken copy, and approving commentary.

For those who do read the topical articles and editorials, there is no mistaking TV *Guide*'s allegiance to the commercial system of broadcasting and the consumer society. Network television is "free TV" and cable television is "pay TV."[11] Proposals for counter-advertising are eyed with hostility. The Federal Trade Commission (FTC), which has to this point kept an open mind on the subject, is reviewed critically in a three-part series entitled "Revolution at the FTC." The views of Clay T. Whitehead, the Director of the Office of Communications Policy (President Nixon's chief advisor on communications policy), are quoted approvingly: "Some people tend to view (advertising) as the means by which an insidious business–advertising complex manipulates the consumer and leads public opinion to goals that are broader than simply purchasing the products being advertised. . . . Some feel that what is being sold to the American people is a consumption-oriented way of life. . . . I think that some of these broader concerns are now motivating the FTC."[12]

Public broadcasting, which has rarely distinguished itself for its courage and scarcely poses a threat to commercial operators, is excoriated all the same by a TV *Guide* author who finds it "unbalanced," characterized by "diatribes" and an "extreme left-wing view," "ideological," and "biased." The writer calls for a purge of its leadership.[13]

In much the same vein, the *Guide*'s editor calls Western European broadcasters to account for showing programs critical of American institutions without providing "proper balance."[14] Television in Eastern Europe, it goes without saying, is ridiculed.[15]

Yet all these messages are secondary to the magazine's chief task of presenting a glamorized weekly vision of commercial TV. From purchase to disposal, throughout the brief cycle of its existence, the near-pocket-sized magazine typifies and extends the fragmentation and consumerism that so well serve the mind management of the corporate economy. Once the "TV week" is over, TV *Guide* vanishes. Less perishable, regrettably, are the psychic marks left on the reader–viewers, which our instruments are still too crude to measure.

The National Geographic: Nonideological Geography

To a child growing up in America, the *National Geographic* is a pervasive part of education. The school library that doesn't carry it is almost nonexistent. Rare is the social studies curriculum that doesn't enlist the services of the *Geographic* to illustrate a point. Countless youngsters have pored over the magazine to find pictures or text for some school project.

National Geographic may not have attained the ultimate success—to have become an accepted household term like Kleenex, Levi's, Coke, or Xerox. Failing that, it has achieved the next best thing: the *Geographic* is regarded as "good for you." Doctors and dentists subscribe to it so that their waiting patients may benefit or, at least, not fret.

The magazine is published by the National Geographic Society, a "nonprofit scientific and educational organization for increasing and diffusing geographic knowledge and promoting research and exploration." The publication first appeared in 1888. A successful undertaking since the turn of the century, the *National Geographic* benefited tremendously from the "soaring sixties." Its circulation jumped 4.5 million in a little over a decade, and stood in 1972 at 7.2 million, making it, as it informs potential advertisers without bashfulness, "eighth among all consumer magazines."[16]

Its solicitation of and success in obtaining advertising seem to create no problems for its tax-exempt status as a nonprofit organization. So too, the substantial revenue derived from its consumer advertising presents no moral threat to its educational objectives. It announces proudly, "In all, we deliver 17 million active, adult readers who have money to do things, buy things, go places."[17]

The *Geographic,* however, is much more than just another mass magazine serving Madison Avenue, though it does that too. Its long history, its involvement with the glamorous aspects of scientific exploration, its thorough penetration of the school and library system and the middle-class home, and, above all, its image as an objective source of geographic–cultural information, make it one of the country's most respected and, therefore, influential para-educational institutions. How well does it fulfill its educational and scientific function and how accurate is its claim to objectivity?

If any subject can be said to be value-free, natural geography would seem to have a very good case. Volcanic craters, deserts, glaciers, the ocean floor, and mountain ranges are hardly matters of social controversy. The *National Geographic* seized on this point and insisted from the outset that it would be a noncontroversial journal, concentrating on accurate reportage of natural phenomena. Yet geography itself is of interest only when social factors create a basis for interest. Iron ore attracts attention, for instance, only after metallurgy, itself an outgrowth of social development, requires a supply of ore.

The origins of the *National Geographic* may best be appreciated by recalling the period of its initial appearance. One unsentimental review of the journal's history, written by Tom Buckley of the *New York Times,* notes: "The turn of the century was an auspicious time for producing a popular geographic magazine. The Spanish–American War and the closing of the Western frontier had led Americans to look outward across the oceans for the first time. It was a period of booming trade, innocent [sic] imperialism and general optimism. Americans were anxious to shoulder their share of the White Man's burden in civilizing their 'little brown brothers' in the Philippines and wherever else duty called."[18]

Frank Luther Mott, in his comprehensive *History of American Magazines,* acknowledges the *Geographic*'s interest in these matters. "In the first decade of the new century there was also much about the American dependencies—Alaska, Hawaii, the Philippines, and the Canal Zone. Several articles on the Panama Canal by George W. Goethals and Theodore P. Shonts were important and well-illustrated."[19]

The *National Geographic* has, since its inception, attracted a very "outward-looking" group of powerful Americans to its self-perpetuating governing Board of Trustees. As the interests of the corporate economy have become worldwide, concern with geography has increased. The Geographic Society's trustees represent and are representative of the Empire. The members of the 1972 board, for example, included: Crawford H. Greenewalt, Chairman of the Finance Committee of Du Pont; Curtis LeMay, former Chief of Staff of the Air Force; H. Randolph Maddox, former vice-president of American Telephone and Telegraph Company; Benjamin McKelway, former editor of the Washington *Star;* Laurance Rockefeller; Robert C. Seamans, Jr., Secretary of the Air Force; Juan T. Trippe, former Chairman of Pan-American Airways; James Webb, former administrator of NASA; and Earl Warren, former Chief Justice of the Supreme Court.

Day-to-day decision-making is in the hands of the Society's officers and the magazine's editors. The Society is run very tightly, and editorial control of the *Geographic* has been held since 1899 by the Grosvenor family.

The National Geographic Society, apart from its product, geography, is indistinguishable from other information-gathering, -processing and -disseminating conglomerates. The Society produces globes, atlases, maps, film-strips, TV programs (a *Geographic* special shown by CBS in the fall of 1971 was entitled "Monkeys, Apes and Man" and informed the audience about man's *true* biological self), motion pictures, books, and a publication for children, the *School Bulletin.* The latter, a weekly 16-page publication, now circulates through personal subscription to half a million children from eight to fourteen years of age.[20] Like other conglomerates, the Society participates in joint ventures that extend the range of its activities. Its TV shows are cofinanced by Aetna Life and Casualty Insurance Company and Encyclopaedia Britannica, Incorporated, "old friends of the National Geographic Society."[21]

This burgeoning multimedia activity typifies the histories of many successful commercial enterprises. Mind management comes into the picture because of the *Geographic*'s special and influential educational–informational position, supported by its claim of social detachment and nonpartisanship. It is a model for packaging consciousness. Ideology permeates the periodical. In form and content, the *Geographic* is an exercise in political management which utilizes skillful presentation, concealment, and omission in varying combinations to advance its outlook, ". . . an implicit belief in the capitalistic, free-enterprise system."[22]

Gilbert Hovey Grosvenor, editor from 1899 to 1954 and then Chairman of the Board until 1966, long ago articulated some of the magazine's guiding principles: accuracy, abundant illustrations, and "avoidance of controversy" (". . . only what is of a kindly nature is printed about any country or people)."[23]

These rules permit the *Geographic* to present the world as an essentially conflict-free collection of nice places to visit, which can be afflicted with "troubles" from time to time. "Troubles" is the *Geographic*'s euphemism for social disorder and class and national liberation conflicts. The world the *Geographic* presents is one that was put together before World War I, a universe in which a handful of Western states dominated global resources and populations. Its articles rarely fail to include a nostalgic reminiscence of the old arrangements, some of which still linger on. Staff editor Volkman Wentzel, for example, in an account of "Mozambique, Land of the Good People," reports: "I came upon yard-thick coral walls, remains of an early Dominican mission. Cacti and vines sprouted from cracks, and a fig tree grew through the stone altar. Tombstones and pieces of a baroque baptismal font lay crumbling—reminders of a bold Portugal in a barbaric land."[24]

Staff editor Jules B. Billard, in a 1970 article about Panama, rhapsodizes over the construction of the canal and the technological feats of the engineers. The United States' role in detaching Panama from Colombia by supporting a separatist movement, in order to secure the concession for the canal, is handled this way:

That zone, a strip 10 miles wide across the isthmus, had been signed over to U.S. control by an infant Panama that had become a nation only 15 days earlier. With U.S. backing it had declared itself independent from Colombia, of which it had been a part since the end of Spanish rule in 1821. . . .

The treaty giving the United States the right to build a canal was drafted and signed by a French engineer, acting as Panama's ambassador. It granted concessions even more liberal than those the U.S. itself had sought in earlier unsuccessful negotiations with Colombia. The terms, as a Panamanian businessman phrased it in a discussion with me one day "have caused resentment for that Frenchman and the 1903 treaty ever since."[25]

The *Geographic* reassures its readership that the Panamanians resent the French negotiator, not the Americans who secured the "liberal" terms. And, to show that bygones are bygones, the author quotes a high official who prefers to remain anonymous: "We may not like some of the things you Americans have done, but that doesn't mean we don't like you or respect you. And we'd a lot rather do business with you than with, well, Communist powers, for example."[26]

In applying the rule of avoiding controversy, speaking only in a "kindly" way about a country, the *Geographic* can be nostalgic about, if not supportive of, the remains of early Western imperialism and at the same time omit or slant accounts of popular struggles against foreign domination or everyday class exploitation inside a nation. Buckley found that, "No *Geographic* article on any state in the Deep South in the past 50 years, for example, has mentioned segregation, malnutrition, the Ku Klux Klan, lynchings, sit-ins, or freedom rides. In 'Dixie Spins the Wheels of Industry,' a regional survey that appeared in 1949, Negroes weren't mentioned at all or shown in a single photograph."

Surveying foreign coverage, Buckley found that, "An article on China in 1948 left out the civil war. 'South Africa Close-up,' which appeared in 1962, took note of the existence of apartheid and quoted the Minister of Information extensively as to the reasons why it was desirable for everyone. It didn't print an opposing view and its pictures showed happy blacks laboring in hygienic mines and, gaudily painted, doing their tribal dances."[27]

Since the *Geographic*'s view of the world denies or overlooks the existence of exploitative social relations either within or between nations (except for Communist states, which are represented unfailingly as models of repression), it is understandable that there is editorial embarrassment when conflicts develop. "Troubles" are invariably "fomented" by "outsiders" who carry the virus of disorder into ordinarily tranquil communities. Thus, *Geographic* reporter Wentzel, in his excursion to Mozambique in 1964, interviewed the Portuguese chief of the Northern Territorial Command and passed along this officer's observation with no comment: "Trouble here can come only from the outside, as it happened in Angola. But this time we won't be caught unaware." The reporter's restatement of this remark is: "Watching upheavals in nearby lands, Mozambique prepares for possible trouble."[28]

The liberation struggle in Vietnam has been a problem to the editors of the *Geographic*. The country was featured extensively in the early phases of the United States intervention. However, as the disaster deepened, the *Geographic*'s attention declined precipitously. The magazine carried three articles on Vietnam in 1965, one in 1966, one in 1967, two in 1968, and none in 1969 and 1970. In 1971, a piece entitled "Lands and Peoples of Southeast Asia" skirted the war as much as possible. Buckley's observation is pertinent: "When a place gets obviously disagreeable enough, though, the *Geographic* simply stops writing about it."[29]

In 1965, when hopes were still high, at least in the White House and the Pentagon, that the civil war could be turned around successfully by American military power, the *Geographic*'s reporter presented the struggle in completely personal terms, making the fighting and violence appear random, senseless, and totally irrational. The NLF fighters ("Vietcong") were portrayed as vague, ill-defined, menacing figures, whose actions were frightening but whose motivations were hard to comprehend. Still, there was hope that the war would end soon and victoriously for the American side. The *Geographic* writer "chased dark thoughts from my mind, for it was Sunday morning again, and I was off to the movie at the French Cultural Center; Walt Disney's "Bambi" with sound dubbed in French and Vietnamese subtitles."[30]

By 1971, the same writer shrugs off the war: "Saigonese lucky enough to own television sets can turn off their worries and tune in on 'Bonanza' or 'Gunsmoke.'" And again, "Saigon takes terrorism—assassinations or the bombing of buildings—in stride, such as traffic accidents."[31]

In the same issue, another *Geographic* writer, in a startling example of wishful thinking, puts the significance of recent archeological discoveries in Vietnam ahead of the civil war in terms of ultimate impact on that land's future: "The overwhelming nature of military events has obscured some astonishing discoveries about the ancient history and prehistory of the people who live there. Yet in the long run these discoveries, primarily archeological, will affect—perhaps more than the war or its outcome—the way we think about the area and its people, and the way they think about themselves."[32]

Clearly, the *National Geographic* prefers to escape into archeology and deprecate social conflict—especially struggle which has as its aim the overthrow of the *status quo*.

The magazine also reveals its preference for the waning era of white Western dominance through a multitude of literary and photographic gimmicks. Buckley noted that, "The *Geographic* has always been willing to show breasts in any color but white. On one occasion, a frolicking Polynesian girl appeared suspiciously fair-skinned. The problem was taken care of in the *Geographic*'s photographic laboratories. 'We darkened her down,' said Melvin M. Payne, the president of the Society, 'to make her look more native—more valid, you might say.'"[33]

In the same way, native Burmese "chatter nervously in the growing darkness,"[34] bringing to the minds of the magazine's readers associations with other jungle noises. Similarly, "orphaned Japanese kids swarm aboard" a United States warship for a Christmas dinner.[35] *National Geographic* writers tend to use the word "swarm" when speaking of Asians.

These are small points, but in a magazine so carefully prepared and edited, with some articles commissioned years in advance, such descriptions cannot be inadvertent.

The *National Geographic*'s fondness for nationalistic imagery and reverence for old-fashioned militarism is pervasive. Scarcely an issue passes without a photograph (in color, in recent years) featuring "Old Glory." Even such a nonmilitaristic activity as shooting rapids assumes a patriotic character when the flag is conspicuously displayed above the raft on the magazine's front cover.[36]

The adulation the *Geographic* lavishes on the United States Navy is perhaps a reflection of the Annapolis ties of its family of editors. In any case, the world's seas are at the disposal of American naval power. In 1959, an article by Franc Shor, now associate editor, entitled "Pacific Fleet: Force for Peace" made these interesting points:

"One of the most powerful striking forces in the history of the world is creating an enormous amount of good will for the United States in the Orient. . . . The aircraft carrier is the backbone of our might in the Pacific: [Admiral Brandley] told me: 'The carrier—plus the power of the press to let everyone know it's there and ready.'"[37] The *Geographic* generously provides the power of the press while the Navy supplies the military force.

In 1965, the vice-chairman of the National Geographic Society's Board of Trustees, Thomas W. McKnew, wrote a piece on "The Four-Ocean Navy in the Nuclear Age." Among other observations, he declared: "The Navy today costs the U.S. taxpayer $14,300,000,000 annually—roughly $126 for every citizen 21 years old and over. It is a bargain at any price." The 656 Polaris missiles the fleet had available in 1965 are described as "656 arguments for Peace." Moreover, "to establish and maintain balances favorable to peace, it [the Navy] must exercise its strength on all seas wherever free man is, or may be, challenged." Finally, in the long tradition of militaristic rhetoric, McKnew argued as follows in a concluding section called "Peace Depends On Readiness for War": "To preserve the peace, it is necessary to be proficient and powerful in the art of war. Control of the seas has determined the fate of nations throughout history. It still does. And that control is in able hands—the hands of the global United States Navy."[38]

Later in the year, no doubt to demonstrate its evenhandedness with respect to the rest of the United States military establishment, the *National Geographic* carried an article by board member and former Air Force Chief of Staff Curtis LeMay, entitled, as might be expected, "United States Air Force—Power for Peace."[39]

The sad thing about all this is that the exposure to geography of a goodly number, probably the majority, of Americans begins and ends with the *National Geographic.* Its reputation as a trustworthy source is enhanced by glowing bibliographic recommendations, of which the following is typical: "Few magazines serve as many audiences and so many purposes as this old standby. It can be enjoyed by the elementary school child as well as by the professional geographer. Its reference value is particularly high, and it is one of the few magazines which should be in every library . . . As one critic put it, this is 'a voyeur's dream . . . for gazing on all sorts of exotic delights.' No more need be said."[40]

Can Americans, with the *Geographic* as their guide, hope to understand, much less empathize with, "have-nots" struggling to break out of centuries of colonial and domestic oppression? "A reader who depended solely on the *Geographic,*" wrote Buckley in 1970, "would have about the same viewpoint as Marie Antoinette achieved from her apartment in Versailles."[41]

Marie Antoinette's world outlook, courtesy of the *National Geographic,* is some preparation for the nuclear age!

"Pure" Entertainment: Walt Disney Productions, Inc.

In 1972 *Fortune* magazine confirmed what had been suspected for a long time—that the Walt Disney entertainment empire is one of America's largest industrial enterprises, ranked 502nd in the nation with sales exceeding $175 million.* [42]

* Sales increased spectacularly to $329 million in fiscal 1972, reflecting the huge revenues derived from Disney World, the new entertainment park in Orlando, Florida. *Los Angeles Times,* 22 November 1972.

To American businessmen this came as no surprise. Indeed, years earlier, they had voted Disney, along with Henry Ford, Andrew Carnegie, John D. Rockefeller, Jr., and other illustrious capitalists as one of the ten greatest men of business in American history. The citation noted that, "while making millionaires of himself and business associates, the Missouri farm boy was entertaining children and grown-ups with wholesome, clean cartoons and live movies . . ." In their opinion, "Walt Disney was a modern day Hans Christian Andersen with business ability."[43] One writer, marveling at the technical ingenuity and size of the exhibits in Disneyland, declared that they "establish [Disney] as the Henry Ford of the entertainment business."[44]

The business, under Disney's direction, reached out to a fabulous and unprecedented kind of market. The eyes and ears, the minds and the bodies, of tens of millions of human beings annually encounter some Disney message or product. Richard Schickel, the biographer of the Disney saga, reported: "In 1966 Walt Disney Productions estimated that around the world 240,000,000 people saw a Disney movie, 100,000,000 watched a Disney show every week, 800,000,000 read a Disney book or magazine, 50,000,000 listened or danced to Disney music or records, 80,000,000 bought Disney-licensed merchandise, 150,000,000 read a Disney comic strip, 80,000,000 saw Disney educational films at school, in church, on the job, and 6.7 million made the journey to that peculiar Mecca in Anaheim, insistently known as 'Walt Disney's Magic Kingdom' in the company's press releases and more commonly referred to as Disneyland."[45]

However inflated by puffery or double-counting, the spread of the Disney influence is impressive. It continues to grow. In 1971–1972, for example, the two entertainment parks, Disneyland in California and Disney World in Florida, attracted 20.3 million customers, "more than the total number of people who attended all National League baseball games played during the same period, and almost twice as many as attended all the NFL football games played during the 1971 season" (*Wall Street Journal*, 8 December 1972).

Disney is not an exclusively domestic entertainment phenomenon. The company's products swell the stream of international communications. As early as the 1930s, Disney comic and story books "appeared in no less than twenty-seven of the world's tongues" and were distributed worldwide.[46] The show "Disney on Parade," which attracted audiences totaling over 7 million persons, in the United States and Canada, has also performed in Australia, Japan, New Zealand, and Mexico City. A two-year European tour commenced in 1972. This production "is introducing the classic Disney stories and cartoon characters to a new generation of children around the world."[47] There are also record clubs, book clubs, and weekly magazines for new readers, as well as encyclopedias that are sold globally.

The corporate structure that manages this vast assemblage of entertainment and popular culture is a model of modern conglomeratization. It oversees domestic and international distribution subsidiaries, a music publishing company, an educational materials company, a research and design affiliate, one enormous unit to manage the newly opened Florida complex, and another to run the hotels in the area. There are also real estate development and communications services affiliates. What makes these enterprises so profitable—first half earnings in 1972 jumped 50 percent over the preceding year[48]—is the skillful utilization of a systems approach to entertainment and especially to the use of the mass media. The company carefully selects one medium to promote its activities in other media, which in turn creates additional interest in the original promotion.

For example, the media preparations preceding and immediately subsequent to the opening of Disney World on October 1, 1971, resembled the logistical planning of D-Day—the difference being that the Disney onslaught was directed at people's minds. The company's annual report observed that "the opening was handled by almost unprecedented newspaper and national magazine coverage, including cover stories in *Look* and *Life*, and major sections in such other magazines as *Time*, *Newsweek*, *Paris Match*, *Epoca*, *Esquire*, *Forbes* and *Business Week*." Most important of all, "An estimated 52,000,000 people across the United

States were introduced to Walt Disney World during a 90-minute NBC Television Special on October 29th."[49]

The effectiveness of television to focus attention on other Disney entertainment and business promotions has been understood and effectively applied by the Disney management since the beginning of television. Disneyland was financially linked in the beginning with ABC–Paramount Theatres, Inc. ABC bought 34.8 percent of the shares of Disneyland, Incorporated, and Walt Disney agreed to produce a weekly TV show, *Disneyland*, for ABC for seven years. Said Disney at the time, "I saw that if I was ever going to have my park, here, at last, was a way to tell millions about it . . . with TV."[50]

When Disneyland opened on July 17, 1955, there was a 90-minute ABC-TV Special, on which dozens of celebrities appeared at the site guided by Disney himself. Disneyland became an instant hit, and so did the weekly TV program.

The company's television revenues are modest in comparison with its other activities—$8 million in 1971,[51] while films accounted for $64 million and total revenues were $175.6 million—but TV is essential for the advertising it affords Disney's films, amusement parks, and commercial products. "The Wonderful World of Disney," now in its nineteenth season, and its eleventh on NBC, remains in the "top twenty" shows; according to the Nielsen TV index, the show's first seven episodes in 1972 reached a total audience of more than 19,000,000 homes.[52]

The interwoven promotions of TV programs, the amusement centers, and new and old films in turn heighten interest in the printed materials of the Disney complex. In foreign markets, the printed products sometimes precede the films and TV programs, and generate demand for these other items. In any case, the way in which film, TV, and print are managed to promote Disney creations and products derived from these creations is a source of envy and admiration in the marketing field. TV *Guide*, for example, discussing a television show that was successfully generating commercial product tie-ins, noted: "The first, and still the most successful, film merchandiser is the Disney studio, which . . .

first began to move Mickey Mouse watches, comic books and related products by the millions in the 30s. Presently, Donald Duck joined the parade . . . Today [they] do $11,000,000."[53]

Business Week had earlier called attention to Disney's adept timing. "The pattern set with Mickey Mouse is followed with the Beatles and James Bond merchandising today. Long before other movie men realized that paperback books help the sale of pictures, Disney Studios was timing comic book distribution to picture release."[54]

Disney's recognition of the associative effects of imagery and the interrelatedness of modern communications is further attested to in Schickel's observation that, "no Disney character is allowed to appear on products with unpleasant connotations for children, such as medicines."[55]

The Disney empire deals largely, though no longer exclusively, in imagery. More recently, as the enterprise has prospered, real estate operations, hotel construction and management, transportation, and communications services have been added to the company's interests. Whereas at Disneyland motel and hotel concessions were from the start granted to outside interests, at the new Disney World the company retains ownership and control of these ancillary but very profitable activities.

Nevertheless, film, television, print materials, and the entertainment parks (themselves thousand-acre assemblages of imagery) remain the dominant elements in Walt Disney Productions. Communications—in all the media—are the entertainment empire's main products. What, then, are the messages that flow from the dozens of feature-length films, the continuing weekly TV shows, the thousands of comic and story books, the educational materials, the records, and the amusement parks themselves?

Just as the Disney management finds it profitable to use a systems approach to sell its products, the best way to understand the message it is selling is to adopt a systems analysis approach to the product—that is, to take the Disney machine as an entity, and to examine its many outputs as *elements in a totality* with some common features. Approached in this way, the message becomes the dominant factor, and the media that carry it appear secondary. It should never be forgotten, however, that repetition and cross-media reinforcement are crucial factors in disseminating the message.

Max Rafferty, a former Superintendent of Public Instruction in California and a very conservative gentleman, has referred to Disney as "the greatest educator of this century."[56] If greatness is equivalent to degree of impact, Rafferty may be closer to the truth than many have ever imagined. Disney from the beginning claimed to be offering entertainment and nothing else. It was as simple as that. His obituary in the *Los Angeles Times*, the newspaper which covered his successes so enthusiastically, significantly repeated this theme: "*His characters knew no politics*, and received affection from the young at heart *of whatever political persuasion or ideology* (emphasis mine)."[57]

But if Disney was an educator, what kind of education was he offering? And when has education ever been separable from a value system? Entertainment is education and education is ideology. Robert Shayon, TV editor of the *Saturday Review*, points out: "Entertainment programs give audiences cues as to what is valued in our society and how to behave. They're really forms of education, of indoctrination."[58]

Disney was a powerful educator. Since his death, Walt Disney Productions has become an even more influential shaper of minds, because it is able to disseminate its entertainment to more people in more ways than had been possible earlier.

We have emphasized the necessity of analyzing the Disney entertainment function in its overall context. Obviously, the character and nuances of the message may differ from medium to medium, from product to product, and from one setting to the next. With these qualifications in mind, it is accurate, I believe, to articulate the transcendent Disney message, transmitted by film, tape, and comic book, in movie, story, and record, in the great outdoors and in suburban scenarios, thus: *behold a world in which there is no social conflict*. There is plenty of violence. There are some "bad guys," but they are individuals, not representatives of significant social divisions. The world is a happy place and the American middle class experiences the world at its best.

Wherever possible, the message is, intentionally or otherwise (it makes no difference), transmitted in natural settings, preferably featuring "that magical screen combination of children, animals and nature"[59]—categories that deny or, in the case of children, minimize social-class relationships. When such relationships are unavoidable, as in full-length situation-comedy films, they are handled by representing everyone as satisfied middle-class consumers. Not content with making people everywhere conform to American middle-class standards, Disney Productions invariably present beavers, bears, lions, and ducks behaving like the folks in the suburbs.

All of this is accomplished with incredible technical virtuosity in photography, engineering, and construction, as well as a perfectionist insistence on verisimilitude in the details of whatever is being presented—a wildlife scene on film, an audio-animatronic model of Abraham Lincoln at Disneyland, or a TV production of Winnie-the-Pooh.

There are times, however, when the Disney fantasy world, ordinarily deliberately insulated from reality, becomes involved with "the world of events." Ariel Dorfman and Armand Mattelart, two young Chilean scholars, have analyzed Disney comic books and made some surprising discoveries. They find racism, imperialism, greed, and arrogance permeating the "value-free" comics that circulate on a mass basis throughout Latin America. More than three-quarters of the stories they read featured a voyage in search of gold. In the remaining 25 percent, the characters compete for money or fame. Half the stories occur in extraterrestrial places, the other half in foreign lands where the people are generally primitive. They are all nonwhite. Only men are shown, and they are predominantly enormous and muscular, except when they are pygmies. They are like children. They don't need to produce to live. They are model consumers.[60]

Mattelart believes that "imaginary childishness [which Disney specializes in] is the political utopia of a class. In all the comics, Disney uses animality, infantilism and innocence to mask the web of interests which form a socially and historically determined and concretely situated system: Northamerican imperialism."[61]

There is no doubt that Disney is a very successful part of the North American business system. More significantly, Disney products influence the mind and the images that move across it. Disneyland is a model for the integration of entertainment, business, and education. Package deals with airlines and bus companies promote excursions to the park from all parts of the nation. Illustrative of its penetration into all levels of life are the park's high-school graduation parties. Capping their studies with a final celebration at the entertainment emporium has become something of an institution for students all over the West. At graduation time in 1972, the park reported that "more than 110,000 high school seniors are expected to attend the seven Grad Night parties at Disneyland this year. New graduates from California, Nevada, Arizona, Utah and Hawaii will attend the parties . . . The Grad Night parties, begun in 1961, have been attended by more than 700,000 persons."[62]

At these final school ceremonies, young people receive a good deal of instruction—but by no means their last—from such educators as Welch's grape juice, Carnation ice cream and milk, Swift's premium chicken, Bank of America, Santa Fe Railroad, TWA, Richfield Oil, Kaiser Aluminum and Chemical, Monsanto Chemical, Pendleton Woolen Mills, Pepsi-Cola, ABC and many other major consumer goods and services producers whose advertising and exhibits are integrated into the park.

While the throngs wander through the self-designated "happiest place on earth,"[63] drinking, eating, and resting at their own considerable expense, they may eventually enter the "Hall of Presidents." Here they will be privileged to listen to a speech of Abraham Lincoln's, which, according to one visitor, ". . . is a surprisingly uncontroversial Lincoln who speaks. In fact, it's a speech that needn't offend any political persuasion whether Robert Welch's or Jefferson Davis'. Lincoln has been redeemed for all America as a nonpartisan President whose rhetoric is reminiscent of General Douglas MacArthur's . . . There is no evidence in his speech of the slavery issue, or the Civil War. This is the Lincoln we can all accept without reservation."[64]

This empty and yet very meaningful message, in terms of possible effects on the audience, tells us what the entertainment that Walt Disney Productions creates is all about—the evisceration of social meaning and the reinforcement of the *status quo*.

Conclusion

Two national magazines and an entertainment conglomerate hardly comprise the informational universe of the United States. Yet they are representative of the main tendencies of, and basic techniques applied to, current information-cultural outputs. The role they claim as nonpartisan transmitters of recreational or neutral information has become one of the distinctive features of the communications flow in America—the specialized channel concerned entirely with one element of existence: e.g., travel, sports, comedy, news, drama, whatever. This is supposed to eliminate automatically the possibility of social involvement and generalized bias. In fact, it more effectively conceals the social premises and assumptions that specialization promotes. Besides, specialization itself is often an indication of some distortion in the social process.

The values and assumptions common to TV *Guide, The National Geographic*, and Walt Disney Productions are identifiable in their contents and their formats. All are satisfied with existing social arrangements locally, nationally, and globally. They view consumerism—the quest for material satisfactions as substitutes for all other human needs—always with equanimity, sometimes with enthusiasm. Self-interest, acquisitiveness, and the goal of individual success, along with a belief in unchanging human nature, are promoted in their materials with unfailing regularity. The feasibility of social alternatives—different ways of organizing human efforts—is denied or, if considered at all, discounted.

The value to the corporate economy of these channels of entertainment and information does not go unrecognized. Walt

Disney received from the very conservative Freedoms Foundation at Valley Forge its highest award, the George Washington Medal, in 1963. Former President Eisenhower, serving as Chairman of the Foundation's Board of Directors, made the presentation and read the citation: "Walt Disney, Ambassador of Freedom for the U.S.A. . . . For his unfailing professional devotion to the things which matter most—human dignity and personal responsibility. For masterful, creative leadership in communicating the hopes and aspirations of our free society to the far corners of the planet."[65]

Walter Annenberg, owner and publisher of TV *Guide* (and a heavy contributor to the Republican Party), was appointed United States ambassador to Great Britain by President Nixon.

The *National Geographic* is treated with reverence by historians and bibliographers. One writes, "There is really nothing like it in the world."[66] Says another: "No other magazine has ever captured the charm of strange and familiar lands more continuously than the *National Geographic*—or with more success . . . the *Geographic* has had few peers through the years. It is a convincing and heartening witness to the supremacy of quality."[67]

But neither TV *Guide*, *National Geographic*, nor Walt Disney Productions has ever received the supreme recognition accorded the *Reader's Digest* on the occasion of that magazine's fiftieth anniversary in early 1972—a White House dinner and party.

The President of the United States, in the company of a galaxy of American entertainers and other luminaries (Bob Hope, Billy Graham, Ray Coniff, James Michener, Sidney Hook), bestowed on the owner and publisher of *Reader's Digest*, De Witt Wallace, this tribute: "He has made a towering contribution to that freedom of the mind from which spring all our other liberties."[68]

If the President can make this assertion, we may well wonder what words await expression at the appropriate time to the managers of the *National Geographic*, TV *Guide*, and the *Disney* operation—whose messages and images continue to serve so well the prevailing institutional system.

CHAPTER FIVE

The Polling Industry: The Measurement and Manufacture of Opinion

> *Of course, we still have mass demonstrations, riots, and rent strikes, but I submit that, without public opinion research, we would have had many more such disturbances, and more violent ones. Indeed, when violent expressions of public opinion occur, we should look carefully at our own performance and ask whether, in some respect, we have failed to do our job. We may be partially responsible for disturbances that interfere with the productive division of labor on which our civilization is based.*
>
> W. PHILLIPS DAVISON
> *Public Opinion Quarterly*,
> Fall 1972, p. 314

BECAUSE AMERICAN SOCIETY is saturated with physical objects, it is natural to think of inventions or technological creations as machinery or machine-related processes, *e.g.*, a new computer, a transistor radio, or a supersonic airplane. Yet there are other kinds of inventions. An increasingly important component of the machinery of mind management is a relatively recent social invention, the opinion poll.

The opinion survey is a means of ascertaining individual and group habits and preferences, which, if the research design is competent, seemingly will afford quite accurate indicators of national (or regional or local) attitudes or choices.

The ordinary durable good, and the technical process that fashions it, generally represents a linear relationship between designer, manufacturer, and purchaser. Once the design has been chosen and the production lines organized, the good is manufactured in quantity, distributed according to the principles of the marketing system, and purchased on the basis of (stimulated) wants and income availability.

It is, of course, true that the character of the institutional structure will significantly affect the kinds of processes and products that are created. Nevertheless, the machinery engaged in the production process is essentially neutral and transferable to other, dissimilar institutional environments. The degree to which such transfers of technique and equipment may modify, or be modified by, their new environments remains a matter of continued interest and inquiry.

The poll/survey is an invention of an altogether different sort. That it utilizes a statistical technique and not a physical process is obvious. Yet it differs from the technological discoveries with which we are familiar in a still more fundamental sense. The poll, though a scientifically shaped instrument, cannot be a neutral construct. By its very nature, it is concerned with human habits and intentions, and its formulation and utilization are inseparable from ongoing social relationships. It is involved at all times with human behavior, individual choice, and social awareness. It is intended to assist policy-making and decision-making at varying governmental, political, and economic levels. To take a poll is itself an act of social policy. To inquire about a group's views, for *any* reason, suggests the initial mind-set of the poll-taker and implies a promise of future action or, no less significantly, inaction, somewhere in the societal decision-making apparatus.

Moreover, though it is not in the goods-production business, polling is very much part of the newly emerged consciousness industry. Its considerable contribution to the production and management of national attitudes will be detailed later in this chapter. One observer noted, not long ago, that public opinion "is being managed on an unparalleled scale" and that "the financial outlays for opinion management are tremendous."[1] The mechanics of sophisticated opinion management in an advanced market economy are heavily dependent on polls and surveys. We are concerned here with (1) the recent history of opinion surveying in the United States; (2) the use of polls at home and abroad; and (3) an appraisal of the role of polls in a socially divided society.

The Origins of the Survey in the United States

Market surveys and opinion polls are distinctive, but relatively recent, features of the informational landscape of developed American capitalism. Polling originated to meet the needs of commerce, and was further refined by the exigencies of World War II. There are today more than two hundred different polls, which sample national opinion on almost every subject imaginable.[2] In addition, hundreds of local polls are concerned with regional choices and preferences. But economics and politics continue to dominate the fields of inquiry.

Since World War I, the rising productivity of industry and the enormous expansion of productive capacity, growing unevenly in accordance with a general system of unplanned enterprise, have created a feverish atmosphere of consumerism in American society. Providentially for enterprise, the appearance of radio in the 1920s introduced—perhaps "subverted" is a better term—a promising new means of communications to marketing imperatives.[3] The character of broadcasting made surveys inevitable. It quickly became manifest that some means had to be devised to discover and analyze the coverage and impact of the commercial messages being transmitted to a huge but invisible and unknown audience. Lazarsfeld, an early observer of these trends, states: "Commercial consumer studies had greatly contributed to the development of sampling methods and had given rise to public opinion polling. Radio had come on the scene and audience surveys were needed to parallel the circulation figures of magazines and newspapers. These data became the raw material for the new field of communications and opinion research."[4]

Paul B. Sheatsley, in his presidential address to the American Association for Public Opinion Research (AAPOR) in 1968, also paid homage to commerce's singular contribution to survey research in referring to the founders of polling (Gallup, Roper, and Crossley) as "those market researchers turned pollsters."[5]

If the requirements of marketing fathered public opinion research and polling, the spur of war provided the second main thrust for the development of survey methods. The onset of World War II produced an assortment of informational needs best met with survey techniques. At first, public understanding of the widening European war, and, once the United States became involved, civilian morale and popular attitudes toward rationing and price control, were continuing matters of great concern to the government. On the foreign front, a wide spectrum of intelligence about the behavior of the enemy and the opinions of the people subjected to enemy occupation were systematically explored.[6] Again, Lazarsfeld reports: "The War brought about a rapid increase of empirical social research in the service of government agencies. Attitudes of the soldiers, morale of the population, and propaganda effects of the government's efforts became the objects of intense concern. A *whole newly developed research fraternity, academic and commercial* carried on this work . . ."[7] (emphasis mine)

The war-induced research created ties between the poll-takers, the government (as far up the ladder as the Presidency itself), and the military bureaucracies, just as the pre-war market research had produced a close and continuing business–polling connection. The associations of survey practitioners with the war effort took many forms. Some of the most prominent poll-takers had direct connections with the armed forces. Elmo Roper, for instance, was deputy director of the Office of Strategic Services the predecessor agency to the CIA, from 1942 to 1945. Hadley Cantril prepared surveys of American public opinion on the war that were brought to the fascinated attention of President Roosevelt, and were considered important aids in helping the president "guide" the nation during the immediate pre-war and early war periods.[8]

Many of the intimate working relationships established during the war between poll-takers and government carried over into the post-war era. The leading American opinion-polling services slipped easily into the national peacetime governing apparatus. It was not remarkable, but almost inevitable, that the major pollsters would offer their talents and resources, unquestioningly and even enthusiastically, to the groups with whom they had worked so closely in the preceding time of crisis.

The nation in 1945 was no longer a state embattled against an aggressive fascism. On the contrary, its own expansionist inclinations were finding expression. Circumstances had changed, but no fine distinctions were drawn. An imposing array of newly achieved informational skill, inside and outside the governmental sphere, was assembled to measure and process opinion in the unfolding era of American hegemony. In this enterprise, survey-takers were in the vanguard.

The American Polling Industry Since 1945—The Overseas Experience

Survey research threw itself wholeheartedly into the Cold War. The survey-taking industry identified itself unreservedly with official policy. George Gallup put the matter bluntly on several occasions. As late as 1962, he noted that, "the only department in which *we* may have an advantage over the Russians is in our research methods for pre-testing propaganda ideas and for measuring their success in use." This being so, he concluded, "five billion dollars spent on today's tanks, guns, and battleships will make far less difference in achieving *ultimate victory* over communism than five billion dollars appropriated for ideological *warfare* (emphasis mine)."[9] Of course this could be interpreted generously as a typical self-serving appraisal, no different from that of any other salesman coming to the government's door with a bundle of goods to dispose of. Yet the record shows that the pollsters did more than talk.

Hadley Cantril describes informational surveys made by Lloyd Free in Cuba preceding the Bay of Pigs invasion and in Santo Domingo before the United States' intervention. Both studies revealed conditions that should have deterred the policy-makers. The issue here, however, is not the rejection of useful poll data by bureaucrats but the activity of the survey-takers on behalf of the United States' foreign-policy initiatives.[10] Another example is Simulmatics Inc., a New York-based research company one of whose directors was the late Elmo Roper, that did research in Vietnam for the Department of Defense and AID.[11]

The Gallup Poll organization, which has affiliates on all continents, systematically probes sentiments in dozens of nations to secure information that may be of value to American policy-makers. One account reports on the "numerous surveys undertaken by Gallup-affiliated organizations around the world," and describes a meeting in April, 1969, at which "the directors of the twenty-six Gallup-affiliated organizations met in Merligen, Switzerland, to report on the mood of the public in their respective countries . . ."[12]

The USIA's heavy use of surveys to, in its own words, "advance America's position abroad" has been explored. Less well known, though by no means a secret, is the widespread utilization of American commercial polling agencies to carry out the USIA's surveys and probes.[13]

Polls by themselves accomplish little. How they are used in the process of directing a people's consciousness is another story.

In the international field, the matter of "advancing America's position abroad" is quite straightforward. When opinion polling is conducted overseas by American commercial survey-makers, either on behalf of the United States Government or for private companies, it performs the functions Gallup assigns to it—pretesting commercial or governmental propaganda ideas and measuring their success. This obviously serves the ultimate interest of the powerful domestic system. There is no other client.

Domestic polling on foreign-policy questions is less clear-cut, but subject to the same influences. Surveys of the opinions of the domestic population about foreign policy questions invariably serve manipulative ends, as Hadley Cantril's account of Roosevelt's use of polling data in 1940–1941 demonstrates.[14] We will return to this subject later.

For issues of domestic policy, the situation is still more complicated. While the differences between the national and international information control systems may be inconsequential, the *appearance* of national diversity makes a pluralism of sorts seem plausible. It is to this phenomenon we now turn.

The American Polling Industry Since 1945— The Domestic Experience

Domestically, the polls' chief function continues to be to provide information on consumer preferences and habits to corporate business. More recently, with the advent of television, the use of political surveys has increased enormously, causing some observers to characterize the alliance of polling with TV as the basis for a "new politics."[15]

Whether applied to commerce or to politics, the survey process provides a remarkable reinforcement for the institutional infrastructure. How could it be otherwise? Those who dominate governmental decision-making and private economic activity are the main supports of the pollsters. The vital needs of these groups determine, intentionally or not, the parameters within which polls are formulated. The support they receive is very real in financial terms, but it would be a mistake, though a very natural one, to regard the survey-makers as a group as no more than a bought service, available to the highest bidder, whatever his ideological perspective. The relationship is more subtle. It is past associations, economic motivations that parallel those of the system, and personal predilections that make the pollsters, by and large, true believers in a market economy. To it they attribute the virtues of freedom and democracy. The possibility that either could exist outside the context of a private enterprise system is hardly considered.

Moreover, the survey research firms reflect in their own operations and organizational structures the basic characteristics of the American economic system. Serving the giants of American industry, the best-known polling companies have either become weighty economic units in their own right, or been incorporated into business conglomerate empires. In the past few years, twenty research firms have been bought up by big business.

Louis Harris and Associates, Inc., for example, now belongs to the Wall Street firm of Donaldson, Lufkin and Jenrette, Inc. Daniel Yankelovich, another survey-maker, was "conglomeratized" by Leasco, an aggressive data-processing company. Daniel Starch and Staff, Inc., is a parent company of Daniel Starch, the market research firm; C. E. Hooper, the ratings outfit; and the Roper poll organization.[16]

The trend to consolidation is likely to accelerate as more American corporations act to benefit from consumer and product attitude surveys in their overseas markets. Already American-owned market research companies occupy a prominent place in the international economy. Britain, for example, is practically home territory for American companies.[17] In addition to Gallup's multinational activities, Louis Harris has two companies in the United Kingdom and plans a Tokyo operation. Daniel Starch and Staff, Inc., has affiliates in Australia and Canada and ambitious plans for further expansion. Daniel Yankelovich is eying Western Europe as attractive territory for his firm's services.

How do the business ties of the pollsters express themselves in the actual polls?

An example, by no means atypical, of the way the process operates is a survey of public attitudes toward television conducted by Roper Research Associates for the Television Information Office (the public relations unit of the commercial National Association of Broadcasters).[18] Though the inquiry touched on many subjects, its basic thrust as a reinforcement of the existing commercial structure of television was revealed in a key question on public attitudes to commercials, the life-blood of television: "Now, an over-all question—Do you agree or disagree that having commercials on TV is a fair price to pay for being able to watch it?"

Not surprisingly, in 1968, 80 percent of the respondents agreed, 10 percent disagreed, and 10 percent didn't know—seemingly an overwhelming endorsement by the TV audience (assuming a statistically valid sample) for the present economic arrangements which support commercial television. There is one flaw, unfortunately, in this empirical *tour de force*. The respondent has been offered no other alternatives when asked to decide on the merits of TV commercials. One can think of other ways to formulate the question. For instance, "Do you agree or disagree that having commercials on TV is too high a price to pay and that a different means of financing might be preferable?" Such a question entertains not only different ways of covering costs but also the possibility of an entirely different socioeconomic basis for American television. Could this account for its absence from the questionnaire?

Another example, also prepared by Roper for the Television Information Office, received this commentary from *Transaction*:

*Seventy-four per cent of adult Americans approve the principle of commercial sponsorship and support of children's television programs, announced a recent press release from the Television Information Office (*TIO*). The news must have come as a source of tremendous relief to the commercial networks, which have been getting a lot of flak lately for their ham-handed efforts at gulling little boys and girls into the bliss of the consuming society.*

TIO *commissioned the Roper Organization to find out what people really thought of those commercials. And what did it find out? Did it discover that, as the headline of the press release announces, "three out of four Americans approve the principle of commercial sponsorship for children's programs"? Sad to say, it did not—as a careful reading of Roper's question shows:*

Now I'd like to ask you about commercials on children's television programs—and I mean all kinds of children's programs. Some people think there should be no commercials in any kind of children's programs because they feel children can be too easily influenced. Other people, while perhaps objecting to certain commercials, by and large see no harm in them and think children learn from some of them. How do you feel—that there should be no commercials on any children's programs or that it is all right to have them if they don't take unfair advantage of children? (*Emphasis* added)

No Commercials 18%
All right to have them 74%
Don't know 8%

The saving beauty of that last clause! A poll-taker's master-piece—to insert as a given that which is in dispute. The Television Information Office makes no secret of its affiliation, which is with the National Association of Broadcasters. The affiliation of Roper Organization is more elusive.[19]

The affiliations and relationships of most of the survey organizations could well stand scrutiny. Apart from their matter-of-fact acceptance and systematic reinforcement of ongoing institutional arrangements, the ties between pollsters and their sponsors quite often seem to transcend simple contractual relationships.

Two examples are illustrative. A poll indicating that most automobile accident victims in Massachusetts are displeased with the state's no-fault insurance law was found to be commissioned and financed by the American Trial Lawyers Association, a leading opponent of no-fault insurance laws. The poll, reports the *New York Times,* was conducted by one of the largest, oldest, and most respected polling organizations, the Opinion Research Corporation of Princeton, N.J.[20]

Again, in 1971, "In defense of the President's refusal to set a date for withdrawal, White House officials pointed to a recent opinion research poll showing that, while 68 percent of those questioned wanted a withdrawal by the end of 1971, 75 percent opposed a disengagement 'that threatens the lives or safety of American prisoners of war.' The poll is believed to have been commissioned by the White House."[21]

Hadley Cantril, in his fascinating book *The Human Dimension: Experiences in Policy Research*, reveals how simple it is to establish tax-exempt, nonprofit survey research corporations with governmental or foundation money. He himself set up four separate corporations: American Social Surveys, The Research Council Inc., The Institute for Associated Research, and the Institute for International Social Research. The first one, American Social Surveys, received funds from the United States Office of Emergency Management in 1940 to conduct "the first public opinion survey ever done in Brazil" (p. 28). Incidentally, Cantril notes in 1966 that the results of that and other studies undertaken at the same time are still classified.

The Institute for Associated Research was funded in 1951 by the State Department to permit Cantril and his associates to make opinion surveys in Holland and Italy according to the best criteria of the Cold War. The findings went to a select group of individuals, including Secretary of State John Foster Dulles (p. 114).

One of Cantril's first studies for the Institute for International Social Research, funded largely with Rockefeller money, was concerned with "people in France and Italy who voted Communist in protest against their situation in life" (p. 115).[22] The relationships of survey organizations are no less instructive. George Gallup, as one example, appears to regard his worldwide organization as an integral part of the American foreign policy-making apparatus. His direct participation in USIA overseas programs gave rise to one incident so blatant that it was brought before the 1970 Annual AAPOR Conference by the association's Standards Committee.[23] It should be noted that no action was taken.

Another polling firm, Daniel Yankelovich, turned up on the Princeton campus in the fall of 1970 to survey student opinion under a contract from the Law Enforcement Assistance Administration of the Department of Justice.[24]

The Survey Research Center of the University of Michigan

conducted a 1969 study of high school seniors' attitudes to military service and their own plans concerning military service, contracted by the Department of Defense. The report collected data on 2,200 tenth-grade boys from 87 public high schools across the country.[25]

And, what is one to think of a survey "on the hopes and fears of the American people," conducted by the Gallup organization for Potomac Associates, Inc., "a new non-profit research organization supported by foundations and other private sources"? The *New York Times* reports further that Potomac Associates was formed in 1970 to "conduct studies into critical issues [and] is headed by William Watts, former staff secretary of the National Security Council in the Nixon White House."[26]

The observations of one research team, explaining the eclipse of West German behavioral science in the 1960s, have a familiar ring: "A good part of the quantitative research analyzing mass behavior (including consumption patterns, candidate preferences, tolerance of political change, and so forth) was financed by or, at the very least, could be used by those trying to manipulate the masses for their own partisan or private benefit."[27]

It is a healthy sign, therefore, that the polls are not entirely escaping responsible criticism. Milton Rokeach, in an invited address to the AAPOR in 1968, commented on "[the] Aesopian Language [which] places both pollster and journalist in the position of bedfellows trying to defend or to reinforce the values of the *status quo* under the guise of publishing objective reports designed to 'inform the public.' "[28]

Polls and Politics

It is widely agreed that American politics have been deeply affected by the combination of polls and television. A recent work claims that "the real combined effects of polls and television have been to make obsolete the traditional style of American politics, and to substitute a 'cool,' corporate–executive style. This is the 'new politics' as it actually is today—purposefully analytic, empirically opportunistic, and administratively manipulative."[29]

This serious study devotes a great deal of attention to demolishing the theory of the "bandwagon" effect of polls—that is, the alleged power of the polls to portray a candidate as a winner or loser and thereby to perform a self-fulfilling function. According to this theory, a candidate shown to be popular and well ahead in early polls will pick up additional strength on the basis of the so-called bandwagon effect; and the opposite will happen to an aspirant who does poorly in the early head-counting. Crespi and Mendelsohn take great pains to demonstrate that the bandwagon effect is not the threat it is made out to be, and their argument is convincing.* But a far more fundamental charge can be leveled against political polls as they have evolved in the United States: that the polls legitimize certain candidates and certain issues, exclude and therefore de-legitimize other candidates and issues, and, perhaps most significantly, define the context of the political process according to their own generally unspecified criteria.

When, for instance, the Gallup Poll asks, "Which of these two men—Richard Nixon or Hubert Humphrey—do you think can do a better job of dealing with the Vietnam War,"[30] we are being abused. The evidence was overwhelming and long-standing in 1968, the time of the poll, that *neither* of these two gentlemen could or would deal seriously with the Vietnamese war. To ask such a question confuses, and distorts reality for, a regrettably large part of the population.

Again, when George Romney, Nelson Rockefeller, and Ronald Reagan are named in polls early in a campaign as legitimate presidential timber, from whom the American electorate is asked to choose its chief executive, some serious questions are raised. Are poll-takers willing shills in a massive con game? Is a poll any more scientific than TV, which openly sells its pitch to the high-

* All the same, the 1972 election campaign certainly raises doubts. The pre-election polls left the unmistakable impression that McGovern had hardly a ghost's chance to win and that, consequently, voting for him was a wasted effort.

est bidder? Is political promotion possible only through the meretricious efforts of those directing access to the media?

Some General Observations

What may we say, then, about the role and importance of opinion polling as it is carried on in the United States and elsewhere? I believe we may justifiably draw these conclusions:

The opinion poll is a social invention that cannot be considered apart from the institutional web in which it functions. In American society today, this means that the opinion survey, however scientifically conceived, is first and foremost an instrument designed for political ends. These ends are not always evident but when and if the sponsorship of a poll is divulged, deductions are sometimes warrantable.

There is occasionally an instance when a poll originates with an "outgroup." Such an exception only emphasizes the pervasively conservative sponsorship and utilization of most polls. An example of an outgroup survey illustrates why it is such a rarity. In March, 1966, a poll was published which indicated that "public opinion was far more amenable to a conciliatory policy leading to negotiations [in the Vietnam war] than was generally thought to be the case."[31] What was significant about this poll, other than its findings—which were generally disputed and certainly ignored—was its origin. It was proposed and paid for by social scientists employed in the San Francisco Bay area university–college complex. Grass-roots-initiated polling of this sort is an expensive business, and there is no certainty that the findings will even be publicized (though, in this instance, they were to a minor extent).

Support for the overwhelming majority of the thousands of polls undertaken each year derives from the familiar institutional mix which we have come to call the military–industrial–academic complex. There are the countless corporation-supported consumer inquiries; there is the difficult-to-identify governmental trial balloon in the form of a set of questions originating God knows where ("Most In Poll Back Required [Military] Service," headline for a Gallup Poll report in the *New York Times,* March 23, 1972); there are the political polls before, after, and between elections; and there continue to be a multitude of university studies whose nature is determined largely by whoever will foot the bill.

The opinion polls are usually justified as providing an effective and indispensable two-way flow of communications between decision-makers—governmental or business—and the public. According to this view, the wishes and inclinations of the public, once ascertained, afford managers and policy-makers the input that permits them to make both rational and democratically based decisions. Hadley Cantril states it this way: "Clearly, democracy requires effective, reliable two-way communications between the governing and the governed."[32] George Gallup makes a similar point. Democracy, he says, is enhanced by the polls, which permit the people's will and views to be periodically expressed. Insofar as their impartiality is concerned, Gallup cautions that "it should be borne in mind at all times that polling organizations are merely fact finding agencies. They have no rightful concern whatsoever with what is done about the facts. In this they perform the same function in the realm of public opinion as the Associated Press, the United Press, or the International News Service in reporting objectively the events of the day."[33]

The two important functions that poll-takers claim they perform are to assist democracy by facilitating a two-way flow of communication between decision-makers and the public, and to provide objective information, based on scientific methodology, to anyone who wishes to use it. Let us consider these claims in turn.

The Two-way Flow of Communications

Do polls really contribute to a two-way flow of communications? Put this way, the question is both rhetorical and empirical. Information does come back to the inquirer, and it can be measured. Is this, however, what two-way communication is supposed to be about? In my judgment, there is, or there should be, implicit in the concept a reciprocity based on at least a rough equality in the relationship between the communicating parties. A two-way flow, in other words, cannot occur if there is a fundamental disequilibrium—economic, political, racial, or whatever—between the two sides. If there are factors which reduce or eliminate the equality of the exchange, the two-way reciprocal flow is instantaneously deflected into a one-directional manipulative or exploitative channel. If the questioner, by reason of place or associational role in the social structure, is in any way able to exert force or power over the respondent, a poll becomes an instrument of potential oppression and coercion.

What are we to think, for example, of an opinion survey financed by a private organization, the Friends of the FBI, which polled 2,500 young people from 14 to 25 years of age, throughout the country, on their attitudes to the Federal Bureau of Investigation? Having received the results of the poll they sponsored, the group concluded that it "underscored the need for a major information program among young Americans 14 through 25."[34]

If we apply the criterion of equality of power between questioner and respondent as a measure of a poll's democratic potential, we recognize quickly that the survey is invariably a mechanism of manipulative control. When corporations sponsor consumer polls to secure product information, or when the TV audience is sampled for its viewing habits, where is the locus of power? Certainly not with the consumers or the viewers! Since the overall context is the profitability of the company, the answers consumers and viewers provide can only be used *against* them, though this use will be represented in totally reversed imagery, *e.g.*, "The consumer is king!" For example, if the TV audience is polled on its preference of styles among competing electric carving knives, the real issue, never considered in such a survey, is whether the items should be produced in the first place.

The argument can be extended. If it is assumed that the survey-taker represents, in one way or another, the dominant layers in a stratified society, his interests are inevitably, except in the cases of insignificant administrative studies, opposed to the respondent's needs. This judgment, of course, rests on a view of a multi-layered society not as a pluralistic entity with an ultimate harmony of interests but, more realistically, as a pyramid with power concentrated at the apex.

For this reason, U.S.-sponsored polls overseas, undertaken by the government (USIA) or business, can only be used to the disadvantage of the weaker state when the overall context is one of inequality between nations. The late Harwood Childs some time ago observed that "for those who wish to lead or guide other people, knowledge of their opinions and attitudes is almost indispensable."[35]

The poll may warn the power structure against certain approaches and suggest that it move by more devious paths to the same ends. When society is structurally divided, leaders and guides have to be carefully sorted out to determine which section of the community is "leading" and which following. One student of public opinion and foreign policy-making comments, "Contemporary scholarship on public opinion and foreign policy repeatedly underlines the capacity of leaders to shape the public opinion to which they are supposedly responsive, and to interpret the opinions they hear in ways that support their own views . . ."[36]

Conceptually, the poll may be a form of neutral technology, but as soon as it is utilized it plays a policy role which serves some (anti-) social objective. The opinion poll has added a new and remarkably supple instrument to the contemporary kit-bag of social controls.

Do Polls Provide Objective Facts?

Do the findings of responsibly-administered polls deserve to be treated as scientific facts, as their supporters claim? We leave aside the numerous egregious examples, many involving some of the most eminent names in opinion surveying, of polls that have resorted to deliberate distortion to secure results gratifying to their sponsors. The question we are seeking to answer cannot be dismissed so easily. It deserves serious consideration because it is closely associated with the critical question of objectivity.

Assuming integrity and scrupulous methodology, can a poll's

data be regarded as scientific? There are at least two related grounds for disbelief. Insofar as empirical behavioral research in general is concerned, one experienced audience researcher concludes: "The fact is that empirical research always implies a conceptualized starting point, whether one is conscious of it or not. The choice of research objects and approach involves a non-empirical valuation. Likewise, a conceptual system is necessary in order to interpret the results and to put them into practice, a system into which the answers given by the empirical research will fit."[37]

Information theory seems to reinforce this judgment. As one observer comments:

There are no "facts" in science; only an infinity of possible differences amongst which to choose, and, one's choice of a particular difference cannot not be determined by one's "hypotheses." The hypotheses of these pages is that knowledge as such has no value. All knowledge, without exception, is instrumental. *In the scientific terms of information theory: information is everywhere, but knowledge can only occur within the context of a goal-seeking adaptive system. If this is the case, then we are required to ask what the knowledge is being used for and by whom.*[38]

Does this not characterize surveying and survey data? The specific information sought in a poll, no matter how objective the questions, is necessarily discrete, selected from a universe of possible information. Without the full realization of context, most broadly defined, the empirical validity of poll data is not only meaningless but dangerous. Rather than revealing, it conceals the actual parameters of the conditions that are supposedly being explored. Opinion polling as practiced in the United States, and wherever United States-affiliated or -influenced survey organizations operate, systematically and perhaps necessarily eliminates the full context of the universe from which the surveys seek to extricate meaningful information. In a word, polling presents itself as a means of registering opinions and expressing choices but, in reality and as it has worked to date, it is a *choice-restricting* mechanism. Because ordinary polls reduce, and sometimes eliminate entirely, the meaningful context that provides the true spectrum of possible options, the possibilities and preferences they express are better viewed as "guided" choices. This has its ironic side, because the chief ideological claim for the American Way, in its decades-old rivalry with the Sino–Soviet type of organizational system, is "freedom of choice." Polling is, not without reason, a favorite referent of defenders of the American system, for it displays the very visible shadow of choice while surreptitiously denying its substance in its restricted information selection process.

Throughout this discussion, the pollsters' assumptions that public opinion *is* measurable and that people *do* possess views, individually arrived at, on a variety of matters, have not been questioned. This is not the place to examine these assumptions with the care they deserve. Still, it must be stressed that polling about abstract social and political issues, given the existing patterns of fragmented information dissemination in the United States and elsewhere, may be the most deceptive trick of all. If individuals have had their reality organized for them by a consciousness apparatus that invades the home as well as the school, how valid can their answers be to questions that further reduce the context of the issue at hand?

One researcher has touched on some of these delicate points in a useful critique of polling methodology in general and, specifically, in the analysis of a poll on attitudes toward Vietnam conducted in 1967. The study showed how thin and limited the real understanding of the surveyed population actually was, while at the same time the poll was reporting strongly held opinions. The author concluded:

The polls, by formulating alternatives for their respondents, and requiring no evidence of thought about the vast range of alternatives submitted to each respondent, had recorded 80 to 90% having "opinions." The real meaning of such "opinions" ranged from polite compliance in the interview situation to degrees of permissiveness, acceptance, and active involvement. But which?

We found that when we adopted standard polling practices that we doubled our rate of opinion-holdings, but when we tested the same individuals on their bases *for holding these opinions we found many unable to cope with the information that* presumably was the basis for the opinions![39]

In 1945, at the beginning of both the nuclear and the polling age, Paul Lazarsfeld observed:

Suppose someone wrote a warning against the activity of physicists: physics is dangerous because it leads to an atomic bomb; obviously the warning would be misdirected. Scientific progress can hardly be stopped; the forms of our social organization need to be adapted to whatever discoveries are being made. The same holds true for polls. The results of well-conducted polls are scientific facts: these can be misinterpreted and misused. But the solution certainly is not the forbidding of polls—rather it would be to give thought to how polls are used and by whom.[40]

"Scientific progress" is no longer the inspirational term it was when this passage was first printed twenty-five years ago. And, as we have seen, polls too are challengeable as scientific constructs. As for giving thought "to how polls are used and by whom," the evidence of a quarter of a century is available and it is overwhelming. It reveals that polls have served democratic ends not poorly but disastrously. They have cultivated a deceptive guise of neutrality and objectivity. They have fostered the illusion of popular participation and freedom of choice to conceal an increasingly elaborate apparatus of consciousness manipulation and mind management. Mendelsohn and Crespi conclude their book, *Polls, Television, and the New Politics,* with these words: "The challenge is to create institutional controls that will inhibit such developments ['manipulation and phony participation'] and foster genuine two-way communications between political leaders and citizens in accordance with democratic principles. That challenge remains to be met."[41]

To this we might add that it is not even being faced.

CHAPTER SIX

Mind Management Moves Overseas: Exporting the Techniques of Persuasion

> *We have all the right connections in all the right places. . . . We're On Top of the World.* Reader's Digest, *Multinational Editions*
>
> World's Best Seller
> Advertisement, *Advertising Age*
> 23 October 1972

> *In more than a quarter of a century since [1945],* Newsweek International *has grown to 35 editions circulated to virtually every country on the globe . . . Today,* Newsweek International *delivers 1.5 million readers every week.*
>
> Advertisement, *New York Times*
> 20 December 1972

A COUPLE OF HUNDRED giant corporations produce most of the goods and services consumed in the United States. Still more concentrated is the control of the informational apparatus. A handful of electronics companies manufacture the hardware and supply the facilities for message transmission. An additional small number of firms, most of them part of larger conglomerates, engage in the actual process of broadcasting and publishing. The entire informational process is skillfully managed by the advertising industry, which receives its revenues from the major national companies that are the big consumer goods and services producers.

The largest national advertisers in 1971, in descending order of size, were: Procter & Gamble, General Motors, American Home Products, General Foods, Bristol-Myers, Colgate-Palmolive, Ford Motor, Sears Roebuck, Sterling Drug, and Warner-Lambert Pharmaceutical. These were followed by Lever Brothers, Philip Morris, General Mills, Chrysler, Gillette, Kraftco, AT&T, Coca-Cola, Pepsico, and R. J. Reynolds Industries.

Advertising expenditures in 1972 totaled $23 billion, of which $13.1 billion were national and $9.8 billion were local. National and local television accounted for $4.1 billion, radio for $1.5 billion, and all newspapers and magazines between them shared $8.4 billions.[1]

Totally in command of the domestic communications circuitry, the multinational corporation—the international extension of the domestic behemoth—now dominates the global economy, and has become the chief organizer and manufacturer of the international flow of communications.

The main characteristics of the typical multinational corporation have been described thus:[2]

Overseas activity—"[a typical corporation] operates in at least six countries and its foreign subsidiaries account for at least 20 per cent of its total assets, sales, or labor force"

Size—annual sales of at least $100 million

Growth and profits—above average

Management practices—it devotes "a high proportion of resources to research and advertising"

Ownership—mostly American

The internationally active corporation is not an altogether new phenomenon, but its extensive involvement in overseas communications is relatively recent. Since the end of World War II, both the volume and the character of international economic activity have changed considerably. A few hundred United States-based companies, the so-called multinational corporations, now own and control private overseas direct investment approaching $100 billion. The massive buildup of private American investment abroad requires no elaboration here. Though American-controlled raw-material and extractive industries have maintained and extended their holdings around the world, the largest part of the postwar American investment flow abroad has been into manufacturing and service industries in already-developed regions and countries (Western Europe, Canada, Australia). The changing nature of investment has affected directly and consequentially both the apparatus and the content of international communications. A trade publication comments thus on this shift of activity in private American investment overseas: "For the international advertiser and marketeer, [for instance,] this means expanded horizons. The shift in investment means a greater concentration by international business on the production of goods and services and a more rapid development of consumer markets. *Hence, a growing emphasis on the advertising and marketing of those goods and services is to be expected*" (emphasis mine).[3]

U.S. raw-material and heavy-goods-producing interests overseas in the pre-World War II days availed themselves of some communications talent to provide their local activities with a favorable image, but such expenditures were marginal at most. Today the situation is entirely reversed. Now the mass media, wherever American manufacturing companies operate, have been summoned to promote the global expansion of American consumer-goods sales and services.

The international community is being inundated by a stream of commercial messages that derive from the marketing requirements of (mostly) American multinational companies. The structure of national communications systems, and the programming that such systems offer, are being transformed according to the specifications of international marketeers.

Advertising requires total access to the mass media. Through the multimillion-circulation magazine, the car and kitchen radio, and the home television screen, the marketing message is disseminated incessantly and effectively. Advertising cannot tolerate, if it wishes to be successful, mass communication channels that exclude its commercials and its commercially oriented "recreational" programming. Therefore, it strives untiringly to penetrate each available communications outlet that has a sizable audience. Advertising's appetite is insatiable, and nothing less than the total domination of every medium is its objective. Once subordinated, the medium, whatever its original attributes, becomes an instrument of the commercial culture.

Accordingly, one measure of a nation's loss of control of its own mass media (apart from the obvious loss through foreign ownership) is the degree of penetration by foreign advertising agencies of the nation's marketing mechanics. "We wonder," reflects a Canadian Senatorial Report on Mass Media, "about the adequacy of laws compelling Canadian ownership of the mass media if the mass media's single greatest source of revenue is controlled from a foreign country, even if that country is the United States—or maybe, in the case of advertising, especially if it is the United States."[4]

Such a penetration also signals fundamental changes in the country's cultural ecology. It indicates a communications structure that increasingly transmits and reinforces attitudes thoroughly compatible with the requirements of the multinational corporate goods producers that are financing the new system.

The emerging pattern is a mixture of economics and electronics that we have seen to be enormously powerful. Sophisticated communications methodologies—those that have proven themselves most effective in regimenting, and securing the attachment of, the domestic population—are being applied internationally at an accelerating tempo. The culture of commerce (or, more precisely, of corporate power) is radiating from its American base in a dazzling display. To sell both its goods and itself, American business abroad employs the familiar services of advertising, public relations, opinion surveys, and market research. And to disseminate the carefully synthesized messages of these bought services, it enlists or subverts the mass media of the many national states in which it operates.

The American Advertising Agency as an International Message-Maker

Advertising has become the indispensable adjutant of the business system, and in its own organizational structure it differs very little from the corporations whose interests it promotes and represents. Advertising agencies illustrate the same concentrated pattern of development as the rest of American enterprise. In 1971, ten percent of the firms in the industry received four-fifths of the domestic business (billings).[5] International billings are much more heavily concentrated.

The major American advertising agencies, much like the manufacturing companies they service, possess resources and obtain revenues that put them far ahead of most of their international competitors. One advertising agency, for example, is about to join the elite group of United States corporations whose sales total $1 billion annually. The Inter-Public Group of Companies (which includes McCann–Erickson) announced its merger with Campbell–Ewald Co. in mid-1972, and comes within hailing distance of this goal.[6] Of the world's ten largest agencies in 1971, only one was not an American firm; of the top twenty-five international agencies, twenty-one were American companies.[7]

The rich domestic consumer market in the United States was the original stimulus for the growth of these word-and-image factories. Its prosperity hastened their initial development. Now they are grazing in pastures far from home. The stupendous growth of directly owned American business abroad has brought with it, of necessity, the marketeers. American factories worth more than $25 billion are manufacturing their products in Western Europe. Another $25 billion worth of American plant is located in Canada. Latin America, Africa, and the Middle

East, though mainly still serving as raw-material depots for Western enterprise, have some American-owned manufacturing capacity, too. The ad men follow their manufacturing clients wherever the potential markets lead, and generally wherever capital investment is made. In 1968 American advertising agencies operating outside the United States had billings exceeding $1.5 billion, a large part (though by no means all) of which was accounted for by their advertising programs overseas. In 1970 advertising expenditures abroad by American companies were estimated at $5 billion.[8]

Who's Where Around the World?

No part of the globe (except, and perhaps only temporarily,[9] the socialist-organized sector) avoids the penetration of the internationally active American advertising agency. A special international edition in 1967 of *Printers' Ink*[10] entitled "Who's Where Around the World" listed forty-five American agencies with hundreds of overseas affiliates. Consider, for example, the far-flung activities of the largest agency in the world, J. Walter Thompson. In 1971, JWT had $774 million in billings, of which $355 million (a sizable 45 percent) originated in twenty-seven countries outside the United States. JWT worldwide has seven hundred accounts and employs 8,000 people in forty-two offices. In some instances it has several offices in one country. It operates in Argentina, Austria, Australia, Belgium, Brazil, Canada, Ceylon, France, Denmark, Britain, India, Italy, Switzerland, Spain, Japan, Mexico, Holland, Pakistan, Peru, the Philippines, Puerto Rico, South Africa (where it has five offices and billings of $10 million), Uruguay, and Venezuela. JWT is the largest advertising agency in seven countries *outside* the United States.[11]

Young and Rubicam, the second-largest American agency in 1971, had $503 million in billings, of which $186 million (over 37 percent) came from the international market. Y&R International now has eighteen offices with 1,446 employees in seventeen countries. As an indication of the pace of ongoing international penetration, six Y&R overseas offices were opened within the four-year period from January, 1965, to January, 1969.

McCann–Erickson in 1971 secured $594 million in billings, of which $361 million (roughly 60 percent) were derived from its international branches. McCann–Erickson has sixty-nine offices in forty-six countries, as well as in Hong Kong and Okinawa. It has a particularly heavy investment in Latin America, maintaining offices in Brazil (nine branches), Chile (three branches), Colombia (two branches), Costa Rica, Ecuador, El Salvador, Guatemala, Jamaica, Mexico, Nicaragua, Panama, Peru, Puerto Rico, Trinidad, Uruguay, and Venezuela.

The expansion of American advertising agencies is accelerating, increasingly bringing foreign competitors under the American umbrella. In fact, as of 1970, only two of the top twenty-five American agencies still did not have overseas offices. By contrast, the Leo Burnett Company, the fifth-ranked agency in the United States in 1969, announced the acquisition of the two largest advertising subsidiaries of the London Press Exchange: LPE Ltd., one of England's largest agencies, and LPE International, Ltd., a combination of nineteen agencies in Europe, Latin America, Africa, and Asia. "It is a natural alliance," said Philip H. Schaff, Jr., chairman of Burnett. "Leo Burnett is strong in the United States and Canada and very weak outside. London Press Exchange is strong outside but very weak here."[12]

Sullivan, Stauffer, Colwell and Bayles has announced its intention to buy a big slice of Lintas, the huge Unilever house agency. The deal hoisted "this conglomerate into ninth place among the world's top agencies," with total annual billings in 1969 around $300 million. Needham, Harper & Steers exchanges stock with Havas Conseil, France's largest agency (54 percent of which is owned by the French government); together with a British affiliate, S. H. Benson Ltd., they maintain offices in eleven European countries, Canada, the Pacific, and the United States.[13] America's twelfth-ranked agency, Dancer–Fitzgerald–Sample, "joined the crowd and moved into the international field" in early 1970.[14] Gray Advertising's 1968 annual report rhapsodized about "co-ordinated globalization" among the twelve countries and eighteen cities served by its "global network." Additional mergers were announced throughout 1971 and 1972.

The internationalization of the American advertising business is an integral aspect of the expansion of American industry abroad. It is the latter's voracious marketing requirements that elicit and support the agencies' worldwide activities. The client list of American advertising agencies operating internationally reads like *Fortune*'s directory of the five hundred largest American nonfinancial corporations, supplemented by a heavy representation of major European companies.

In Canada, for instance, most of the revenues of commercial radio and television broadcasting come from the giant American companies operating across the border. In 1969, the top ten broadcasting advertisers were General Motors of Canada, Procter and Gamble of Canada, Canadian Breweries, General Foods, Imperial Tobacco of Canada, Colgate-Palmolive, Ford Motor Company of Canada, Lever Brothers, Government of Canada, and Bristol-Myers of Canada.[15] The tenth-ranked American advertising agency, Ogilvy and Mather, 40 percent of whose income is earned outside the United States by thirty offices in fourteen countries, notes that it serves twenty-four clients (among many others) whose businesses they represent in three or more countries.[16]

J. Walter Thompson, successful in penetrating five continents for its billings, has practically taken over the informational activities of the Nixon administration as well. One trade magazine, inquiring whether the "White House [was a] branch of J. Walter Thompson,"[17] observed that five former employees of the agency were now working on the White House staff, including H. R. Haldeman, chief of staff to the President, and Ron Zeigler, the presidential news secretary, who used to handle the Disneyland account. Internationally, JWT notes in its 1969 annual report that "we have been retained by the British Government to aid in the introduction of the new monetary system [and] in India we are engaged in a campaign designed to spread information about planned parenthood to the people."

The saturate advertising message, jarring or insinuatingly effective, is now in international communications. The mass media are ideal instruments of transmission—especially television, which captures the viewer in his own allegedly secure living room. The media, if they were not initially commercial (as they were in the United States), end up eventually as business auxiliaries, particularly in the less-developed countries. The lure of advertising revenues is too tempting. Furthermore, the business system cannot permit as influential a "sales tool" as radio–television to function noncommercially, free to refuse to transmit consumer messages.

In the developed countries, long-standing national sovereignty, powerful domestic business interests (some of which resist foreign penetration), and sometimes a tradition of concern for cultural integrity combine to oppose the advertising invasion—but generally serve only to slow it down. Actually, in the high-income nations, a sizable domestic business structure functions as a preparatory internal agent for international commercialism.

It is no surprise, therefore, to discover that American advertising agencies have made deep inroads into most of the already industrialized states. In Great Britain, for example, "the situation now is that of the top twenty London advertising agencies, only seven are totally British. All the rest are American owned, or, in a few cases, have strong American links. In the top ten, the U.S. dominance is even greater, with only two of the ten retaining total independence."[18] In West Germany, France, Italy, and even Japan, American advertising agencies now account for the bulk of national advertising. In the Western European Common Market as late as 1972, with the exception of two French advertising firms, "the only European-wide agencies [were] branches of American concerns."[19] The other side of the world is experiencing the same loss of national control of the image-making apparatus. A report from *Advertising and Newspaper News* notes, "Overseas agencies gain whole or partial control of 15 of 24 largest Australian ad agencies and Australians berate themselves for lack of self-faith."[20]

In many of the less-developed states, the control of internal communications by foreign (generally American) business interests is often overwhelming. *Le Monde* reports, for example, that in Peru before the accession of the current military government, "more than 80 per cent of the advertising carried by Peruvian newspapers, radio and television is channelled through big American advertising firms, such as J. Walter Thomson [sic], McKann Erickson [sic], Grant Advertising and Katts Acciones, Inc."[21] Venezuela is even more monopolized by American agencies. A similar pattern, varying in degree, applies in Rhodesia, Kenya, Nigeria, India, Malaysia, Pakistan, Thailand, and many other low-income nations.[22]

Advertising and the mass media that it eventually traduces are, therefore, the leading agents in the business of culture and the culture of business. Other services such as public relations, marketing research, and opinion surveying, all of which are utilized to make the marketing effort more effective, further feed the stream of international commercial communications.

Public Relations as an International Information Source

Public relations, a practice of American business since the early years of the twentieth century, has also become an international phenomenon following the migration of American capital abroad. Compared with the growth of international advertising, PR is still a rather modest, but steadily expanding, activity. A recent estimate put the foreign PR expenditures of American companies at $50 million.[23] Whereas advertising commonly aims to sell the corporation's output, PR's goal is to sell the company itself—as useful, productive, and beneficial to the society in which it is located. As American capital floods a country and wrests control of key industries, this is no mean task. Here is the problem as seen by the executive vice-president of Hill & Knowlton, the most important American company engaged in international public relations:

Let us review the situation confronting the American corporation today in Western Europe: For a time following World War II, American companies found European countries eager for dollar investment—and the markets seemed almost limitless. In the *past decade or so, American business responded with a tremendous increase in direct U.S. investments in Western Europe. In 1965 the total approached $14 billion, compared with $1.7 billion in 1950* [closer to $25 billion in 1972].

In recent years the climate has changed: the "welcome" sign has been replaced with one reading "Yankee Go Home!" A recent survey by Opinion Research Corporation disclosed considerable pressure to restrict the growth of U.S. firms in four Common Market Countries. Fifty-six percent of the business men [emphasis mine] *in Germany believe their government should discourage U.S. investment. For Italy the figure was 44 percent, France 40 percent, and the Netherlands, 31 percent.*

. . . . Under these circumstances, American corporations face difficult problems. They cannot merely withdraw—they must work harder than ever—and much of their attention must be given to the public relations aspects of their international operations.[24]

Or, put otherwise, it is the task of American corporate-supported public relations to overcome widespread resistance to American penetrations of other nations' economies.

The manipulation of symbols to achieve this objective is accomplished skillfully, generally unobtrusively, and intensively by the professional image-makers. As one business bulletin noted, "Worldwide PR is, quite simply, the art of using ideas and information through all available means of communications, to create a favorable climate of opinion for products, services, and the corporation itself."[25]

When PR has its way, the public is repeatedly exposed to promotional messages for the sponsoring company or complex, or even the entire business system, from an unidentifiable source. Years ago, an American business periodical observed:

As expert communicator, PR *plays a unique and quite startling role in the whole flow of communications between the business community and the public. This role is often glossed over, but the simple fact is that much of the current news coverage of busi-*

ness by the American press, radio, and TV *is subsidized by company* PR *efforts.*

. . . . [O]ne hundred thousand public relations practitioners serve as a tremendous source of communications manpower. Without them, only a handful of newspapers and radio or TV *stations would have the staff or resources to cover business activities . . .*[26]

Emphasizing the fanciful means that are required to promote modern business, a later study concluded:

The relative significance of public relations cannot be gauged by estimating total expenditures for this work. We have no such estimates, and the figure would probably be small in comparison with advertising proper. The most telling test of the significance would be to determine the portion of the contents of our newspapers [and television and radio programming] that has originated from public-relations offices. This portion is probably quite remarkable.[27]

In this curiously inverted state of affairs, the public is supposed to benefit from privately prepared press releases that are fed into the mass media, because the latter would be unable, if left to its own resources, to produce enough such material. Now the international community is receiving these benefits as well. *Business Week*, a decade ago, estimated that "among the top three hundred companies in the country, three out of four have full-fledged PR departments, a broad jump from the one out of fifty reported in 1936. New corporation PR departments are starting at the rate of one hundred a year."[28] The top three hundred companies, it may be recalled, are the major exporters of capital and the main owners of overseas plants and facilities. In a survey undertaken by Opinion Research Corporation in January, 1968, the five hundred largest industrial corporations listed in the *Fortune* directory were asked to fill out questionnaires about their foreign public-relations programs. Only 153 replies were received and, of these, forty-three reported no overseas PR activities. The survey, therefore, represents the self-selected response of 110 major American companies engaged in foreign public relations. The basic findings with respect to these firms were summarized thus:

. . . *The number of companies engaging in international public relations activities has increased markedly in recent years.*
. . . *These companies are carrying out public relations programs on every continent and in every major country.*
. . . *The programs are usually handled by staff members based in the overseas countries.*
. . . *Only one-third of the respondents use either a public relations firm or advertising agency to implement their overseas public relations programs.*
. . . *The principal activities are press releases, product publicity, and exhibits and special events.*

Other activities include community relations, employee relations, and government regulations. *Public Relations Quarterly* sums up the study in these words: "Not only are more companies entering the overseas public relations field, they also seem to be more active."[29]

Though most of the major American corporations active internationally use their own staff for public relations work (General Motors has a several-hundred-man PR corps spread around the world),[30] some rely on the efforts of companies organized exclusively for that purpose. Accordingly, American public relations firms, much like their ad agency rivals, have organized subsidiaries and affiliate relationships abroad.[31]

To recapitulate, the overarching aim of international PR is to make American corporate penetration palatable, or at least tolerable, to the host areas abroad. In the Latin American countries, Anaconda, Braden, Braniff, Chrysler, Du Pont, Esso, Ford, General Motors, W. R. Grace, Kaiser, and Pan American Airways "are all too conscious of the tremendous importance of keeping a regular flow of communications with local publics as a means to gain their acceptance, understanding and esteem."[32]

National and local mass-media systems are infiltrated by business messages not necessarily identified by their sources of origin. Hill and Knowlton even prepared a guidebook to familiarize less knowledgeable PR men with the techniques of overseas promotion; the local media have the highest priority.[33]

With the advent of space communications, the opportunity to achieve a worldwide audience for promotional ends has not been ignored. In June, 1969, for example, the space satellite system was used to herald the opening of an iron ore complex in Australia, owned and operated by an American multinational corporation in association with other business companies. "Coordinated planning, American techniques and Intelsat make Australian mine opening a world event," reported *Public Relations Journal*.[34]

It may seem superfluous to add that the ultimate goal of all this communications activity is control of resources and markets that will produce profits. Sometimes this simple but consuming aim is overlooked. It is useful, therefore, to reflect on some PR wisdom from a man who was a partner of Ivy Lee, the cosmetician for John D. Rockefeller. T. J. Ross, in a talk in 1961, observed:

A public relations man is not worth his salt if he succumbs to "pie-in-the-sky" thinking divorced from the realities of his business. And he will not stay long on the management team if he does. In his zeal to place his corporation in the most favorable public light, he must not forget that a business is first and foremost a profit-making enterprise, not an eleemosynary institution. In the relationships he seeks to create between the corporation and its publics he may be soft-hearted, but he must not be soft-headed.[35]

The Opinion-Takers and the Marketing Researchers

Two other media-related services supplement the information-generating business that engages so much of the attention and resources of American companies active in international markets:

the opinion survey organizations and the market research companies.

Opinion polls are generally considered part of the contemporary political infrastructure of parliamentary–electoral societies. In fact, by volume and in the character of the work, market–economic undertakings account for a substantial part of the polltakers' overall business. The distinction between surveys and market research is often extremely thin, and the techniques of uncovering political attitudes and desires may serve to orient economic activities and policies. For example, the Opinion Research Corporation recently announced the establishment of a new company, Market and Opinion Research International (MORI), with headquarters in London. This is a joint venture with NOP Market Research, London. MORI, the new outfit, is expected to provide facilities for research in North America, the United Kingdom, and Europe.[36]

The Gallup Organization, the best-known American opinion-surveying company, identifies itself as providing "marketing and attitude research." Gallup International, which includes its autonomous overseas associates in a loose network of affiliate relationships, "covers 36 countries or regions throughout the world. It undertakes surveys on a world-wide or European scale in the fields of marketing research and of public opinion and behavioral sciences, to be conducted on a contract and client basis."[37]

A. C. Nielsen Company, the major market research company in the United States, engages in surveys as a matter of course; it operates in twenty different countries on four continents. It supplies some research services to eighty-six international organizations with parent companies located in eight different countries. Its television audience research services have been established directly in Canada and Japan and, through joint ventures, in Ireland and West Germany. This rating service, which creates frenzy among commercial TV broadcasters scrambling to achieve high viewing ratios, is described by Arthur C. Nielsen, founder of the company, thus: "Since this type of research exerts a significant and favorable effect on the efficiency of one of the most important methods [television] of moving goods from producer to consumer . . . it is lowering the cost of distribution and creating increased profits for manufacturers and greater values for consumers."[38]

The view of television as a "method of moving goods from producer to consumer" explains, of course, the pathetic condition of television in the United States. The "increased efficiency" that the medium provides for the marketing function can be balanced against the human dysfunction imposed on its audience.

Other firms also have worldwide surveying operations. International Research Associates (INRA) conducts market and opinion research in the United States, Latin America, Europe, Africa, the Middle East, Southeast Asia, and the Far East. The company has a network of associated research organizations operating in more than forty countries and principalities around the world.[39] Gallup International conducts periodic omnibus surveys, financed by anyone who will foot the bill, in Argentina (bimonthly), Australia (bimonthly), Austria (quarterly), Belgium (weekly), Chile (bimonthly), Great Britain (weekly), Greece (biweekly), India (quarterly), Italy (quarterly), the Netherlands (weekly), Norway (monthly), the Philippines (annually), Sweden (monthly), Switzerland (quarterly), the Union of South Africa (bimonthly, and limited to the "European" adult population), Uruguay (bimonthly), Vietnam (quarterly), and West Germany (monthly).

The opinion survey, whether conducted under internal or foreign auspices (no easy matter to ascertain), is ostensibly "designed to obtain information, not to create it."[40] In fact, however, it often creates not only information but also the *attitudes* that it is supposed to poll. The problem lies not with faulty sampling or poor interviewing; the questions can be phrased with complete objectivity. Deficiencies in these matters can and do appear but, with increasingly sophisticated polling techniques available, technical errors are likely to be minimal among well-established organizations.

Opinion surveys conducted for American corporations or governmental information agencies present a twofold threat to the societies in which they are undertaken. The polls are structured commercially, and, when their results are published as national sentiment, they cannot fail to aggravate the marketeering influence in the nation by still further legitimizing existing inclinations to consumerism. Of more moment, perhaps, they probe surreptitiously for opinions that may determine or increase the scope of American official or private information-makers' future policy in that country.

Consider, for example, this account of the polling techniques of the USIA overseas:

> *The backbone of the research program [of the* USIA*] is the public-opinion poll, conducted in every area accessible to communications researchers . . . One thing the polls have in common is that they are not openly conducted on behalf of the U.S. Government. A typical procedure is to hire outside firms, generally located in the countries to be surveyed, to conduct research. People who are interviewed know only that a private polling organization is asking them questions. It is felt that knowledge of the government's connection would compromise survey results, so this has been strictly observed.*[41]

In many advanced industrial market societies, locally sponsored market research and polling occur alongside of, and sometimes without competition from, American-supported operations in the same territory. To the extent that these efforts are independent,[42] they provide for their domestic sponsors the same methodology of control and manipulation that they afford their American counterparts. The imposition of a value structure riddled with commercialism is easier in societies already prepared by such practices.

American Business Consultants and Brokerage Offices Abroad

In this far from exhaustive overview of the business-generated information flow emanating from American enterprises abroad, a brief account of private American management-consulting firms and American brokerage offices outside the continental boundaries is relevant and instructive.

According to a recent survey by *Fortune*, the European market for American business advice is lush and still growing. "Over seventy U.S. consulting organizations have stepped into Europe's ripe climate . . . [and] the real invasion has only just begun."[43] *Fortune* lists McKinsey and Company; Booz, Allen and Hamilton; A. T. Kearney; Arthur D. Little; and Leasco as the most active firms currently, noting that they went to Europe initially to serve American multinational companies setting up plants or acquiring subsidiaries there. Now they are attracting many European businesses and organizations as clients. McKinsey, for example, secured the unprecedented assignment of studying the administration of the Bank of England, "the first time in its two hundred and seventy-four years that the Old Lady of Threadneedle Street had opened her arms to a foreigner."

American management methods are not being exported just to Western Europe. They are penetrating, among other places, North Africa. One report reveals that "working quietly in Algerian Government offices or in state-run companies are representatives of such American concerns as Arthur D. Little; Price, Waterhouse; Booz, Allen and Hamilton; Arthur Anderson; and McKinsey . . . the management techniques being instituted are Western."[44]

What is the significance of this highly specialized business communications flow? Since it is entirely confidential, no one knows with certainty. *Fortune* describes McKinsey's activity as having "an aura of mystery: the work is often hard to define in advance, and even harder to appraise in retrospect." *Science*'s European reporter, D. S. Greenberg, concurs: "What McKinsey tells its clients and what, if anything, they do about it is difficult to discern."[45] Yet the general thrust of its advice, he believes, is familiar. Greenberg quotes one American consultant addressing a European marketing conference:

The traditional thrift of Europeans . . . has been replaced by an eagerness to spend and a willingness to go into debt. There is a growing dissatisfaction with the old and the established, and an intense desire to improve, experiment, to try new products and services—to demonstrate affluence. Europeans have even recently come to believe in planned obsolescence. . . . Consider the impact of television. Both the commercials and the programs themselves flood the consumer with new products and a vision of a better living standard . . .

Greenberg remarks, "the efficiency of American industry is not unrelated to the social irresponsibility with which much of it has been permitted to operate, and, whatever it is that the consultants are whispering into the ears of their European clients, it is to be hoped that there is someone else around to point out that making more, cheaper and faster, is not the whole answer to making life better."[46] Given the rising tide of information generated by American business abroad, countervailing voices are less and less likely to find outlets in their own media.

One additional flow of business data can be identified. The internationalization of capital and the magnetism of the American securities market (which provides liquidity to easily unnerved and affluent foreign investors) have occasioned the spread of brokerage offices, investment advisors, and mutual funds abroad. In a recent report, a Bache and Company employee attributes this trend to direct wire connections and computerized information systems: "We can give the investors a faster and more complete story on the market or an individual company than anyone else. An investor in Amsterdam can get information on a U.S. stock faster than he can on a stock listed on the local exchange."[47]

Accordingly, share quotations now move across oceans by cable or satellite,[48] and American stock exchange firms have overseas offices in scores of exotic locations: Kuwait and Saudi Arabia (each has an American branch office); Nassau in the Bahamas (one); Belgium (thirteen); Austria (one); Brazil (two); Canada (thirteen); England (twenty-five); France (twenty-five); West Germany (seven); Greece (two); Holland (eleven); Hong Kong (six); Italy (six); Japan (two); Lebanon (five); Liechtenstein (one); Monaco (three); Panama (two); the Philippines (two);

Puerto Rico (three); Spain (four); Switzerland (twenty-five); Uruguay (two); Venezuela (four); and the Virgin Islands (one).[49]

American Business and the World Market

The economic power of American corporate capitalism has long been manifest. Its postwar global expansion has made it an international system that affects, and is affected by, national decision-making in scores of countries on all continents. Its economic impact is, if not thoroughly documented, at least generally recognized and involves raw material flows and explorations, balance-of-payments conflicts, dividend and profit repatriation pressures, migrations of human talent ("the brain drain"), currency and gold speculation, and shifting shares of world markets. The political consequences, too, of the international operations of American companies are beginning to be appreciated. Instabilities or tensions in local political structures are sometimes correlated with inflows of American capital.

Only the cultural–information sphere has gone almost unacknowledged in the appraisal of America's global influence. Yet, today, control of human beings and of societies requires, before anything else, the manipulation of words and images. Whatever the degree of raw power that can be brought to bear on a people, it is unavailing in the long run (which may not be so very long) unless the dominating society can make its objectives seem, if not attractive, at least benign to those it seeks to control. The methods and messages of communications, therefore, are the most significant and indispensable instruments of modern power-wielders. The attitudinal state of a population helps to determine its political behavior. And beliefs and opinions are remarkably vulnerable to the sort of mass manipulation that the American system of power practices with fantastic dexterity.

Commercially produced entertainment and recreation are the chief carriers of the values and life styles of American corporate capitalism, but the information generated directly by the sizable American business community abroad is also imposing and far-reaching in its effects. It is difficult to overstate the impact of the promotional and "research" activities of large corporations on peoples subjected to them. Moreover, since the agent of influence is often unrecognized, it is both more powerful and less measurable.

The business-financed and commercially saturated communications disseminated through the mass media are aimed at protecting the physical operations of American enterprises abroad and fostering the values and attitudes of privatism and consumerism that are the ultimate supports of the business system. Few are the regions free of American commercialism. The culture of American business is enveloping everything in its path by appealing to individualistic instincts while it reinforces its messages with the imagery of technological gadgetry and consumer delights.

It derives strength also from its utilization of two of the strongest human desires: the yearning of people everywhere for an end to warfare and an acknowledgment of universality, and the equally powerful popular impulse to individual fulfillment. Accordingly, the rhetoric of corporate communications makes much of internationalism and freedom of the special sort that maximizes private benefits.[50] The identification of human freedom with property ownership and the classification of the worldwide activities of business corporations as an inspiring model of internationalism are the chief ideological underpinnings of today's business-originated messages. The advice of Tom Sutton, executive vice-president-international of J. Walter Thompson, on this subject is forthright: "I believe it is the job of international organizations such as [the] International Advertising Association and the International Chamber of Commerce to preach the gospel of freedom and to see that the best systems of control and restraint—in areas where they [sic] may have to be some—are exported for adoption elsewhere, and not the worst."[51]

On the internationalist theme, Robert Sarnoff, chairman of the board of RCA, the electronics super-corporation, invokes the image of a boundary-free world, accessible to everyone but especially to the undertakings of the few hundred multinational corporations. In a call for a "global common market of communications," Sarnoff enthusiastically recommends reducing national responsibility in communications so that it can be considered a "global resource." Such a development, he claims,

would foster an increasing worldwide flow of information that would bring benefits as tangible as the increasing trade among the countries of Western Europe. The distribution of knowledge by such a system would provide greater stimulus to growth than any conceivable program of economic aid.

For the public of all countries, it would provide entertainment, cultural and informational programming from abroad as a routine rather than a rarity. . . .

As data transmission becomes less and less expensive, we will see greater use of computerized controls and even long-distance time-sharing to strengthen the multinational firm as a vehicle for the transfer of technology. The increases in production and productivity, resulting from the global surge of business information, could parallel the economic advances made in the common market over the past 20 years.[52]

All this would apparently occur in the absence of genuine international structures of control and alongside diminished national authority. The beneficiaries, in this context, could only be the giant transnational corporations.

Economic output, technological mastery, and military power have been the traditional strengths of the American corporate economy. Now increasing reliance is being placed on communications control. The heavy informational flow produced and supported by American companies abroad makes a powerful contribution to the domestic maintenance and global extension of the business system and its values.

CHAPTER SEVEN

Mind Management in a New Dimension: From the Law of the Market to Direct Political Control

> *Fundamental to our way of life is the belief that when information which properly belongs to the public is systematically withheld by those in power, the people soon become ignorant of their own affairs, distrustful of those who manage them, and—eventually—incapable of determining their own destinies.*
>
> RICHARD M. NIXON
> *New York Times*
> 22 November 1972

THOUGH WE WOULD LIKE TO BELIEVE that "free men" have existed in some distant time or clime, restraint and suppression of most human beings have always been the rule. It has been achieved in different ways, depending on the character of the society, the state of the arts of suppression, and the resources available to those in control. The main objective generally has been to reserve as much of the social product as possible for a privileged minority, while leaving enough to insure the continued labor of the less fortunate majority. Scarcity, abetted by physical coercion, was the most dependable regulator of human conduct for thousands of years. In the last few centuries, coincident with the rise of modern industry, a more sophisticated system of control and subordination has developed. The emergence of the market society has permitted a relatively unfettered social condition, but one which has left ordinary working people totally dependent on a wage income derived from ever-uncertain employment.

Though this form of industrialization has not yet penetrated every corner of the globe, it is already changing the character of those places in which it has reached its highest development. In the United States especially, and increasingly in Western Europe and Japan, the industrial state is moving, if not onto an entirely new course, at least in a direction significantly different from that which it traveled during its early growth and maturation. The productivity of labor has soared, and the enlarged social product, reflecting the anarchy of its creation, has become increasingly indigestible, though still extremely unevenly distributed.

At the same time, with greater awareness of its weaknesses and needs arising from the social disasters of the first third of the twentieth century, the Western industrial system has reluctantly sought and accepted state intervention to keep it functioning without calamitous interruptions. With increased regulation and control there have developed governmental bureaucracies and an ever-widening stratum concerned with maintaining economic (and political) equilibria. The advanced system has brought with it, also, a heavier reliance on technology and on those trained to invent, produce, and work with the more complex equipment and processes.

After the Second World War, the American economy became the first in which a larger proportion of the labor force was employed in services than in production. Clerical, sales, managerial, and service workers now outnumber manufacturing, agricultural, and other production workers. The trend is continuing, if not accelerating; and the consequences, in the first appraisal, seem more psychocultural than economic.

Peter Drucker describes the employee in this new situation as a "knowledge worker . . . the successor to the employee of yesterday, the manual worker, skilled or unskilled." Drucker notes that "this is a very substantial upgrading," but, he believes, "it also creates an unresolved conflict between the tradition of the knowledge worker and his position as an 'employee.' "[1]

This, according to Drucker, creates serious problems because the knowledge worker "sees himself as just another 'professional,' no different from the lawyer, the teacher, the preacher, the doctor, the government servant of yesterday. He has the same education. He has more income."[2] Yet he remains an order-receiver, filling an obscure box on an organization chart and disenchanted with the narrow options, beyond income, that his extra education has afforded him. Furthermore, he is more cognizant than his earlier counterpart of at least the general contours of his cultural condition. There appears, consequently, a very new dilemma in the advanced market-directed industrial state. Drucker puts it this way:

> *The clash between the expectations in respect to knowledge jobs and their reality will become sharper and clearer with every passing year.* It will make management of knowledge workers increasingly crucial to the performance and achievement of the knowledge society (*emphasis mine*) . . . *It is likely to be* the *social question of the developed countries for the twentieth and probably for the twenty-first century.*[3]

Curiously, Edward H. Carr, viewing the same industrial scene from what might be loosely termed a socialist perspective, comes to a conclusion that is not incompatible with Drucker's. But Carr hopes for a less manipulative future. He writes:

> *The social habits and labour incentives of the pre-industrial period cannot be resumed. But all that we have yet succeeded in doing is to destroy the philosophy, habits and incentives which for a century past have made the wheels of industry turn, without putting anything in their place. The task ahead is nothing less than the creation of a new philosophy which will furnish an incentive and a reinforcement for a new social habit of work.*[4]

For Drucker, who seems not to be unhappy with the social order, the task ahead is one of applied psychology. Carr's hopes rest ultimately on a fundamental restructuring of society's purposes and organization.

The instrumentalities for "managing" knowledge workers are, Drucker acknowledges, still to be forged. But, significantly, the means for handling manual workers and not-so-highly educated groups in the advanced industrial state are very well known, very effective, and continuously applied. The mass media, with radio and television leading the way, are enormously powerful levers of manipulation and control over the traditional working force in the United States, and apparently in Western European industrialized economies as well. Moreover, the evolution of the industrial state to a condition of total automation and computerization, with only knowledge workers in the labor force, is still many decades away. A numerically significant conventional working force continues, therefore, to be processed daily in the mass thought of the prevailing order. And advertising, which has stimulated wants so effectively (and thereby encouraged labor to work overtime for the satisfaction of those wants), undergirds the powerful standard-of-living ideology that provides mass support for the industrial system as it now operates in the United States.

The entire informational apparatus—from the mass media conduits of commercialism and the opinion polls run largely by marketeers to the formal educational system and paraeducational structures—functions to create popular acceptance of the goals and values of the "goods economy." So remarkably successful is this undertaking that it requires the careful attention of the viewer or listener to detect when the selling message ends and the "recreational" material begins in most broadcast programming. Some observers of the social scene are doubtful that this omnipotent conditioning can be overcome. George Lichtheim, for example, denies that the working class has been "corrupted" by "the desire to possess consumer goods," but nevertheless concludes that equality and social decision-making are not highly prized by the popular majority, who are instead "overwhelmingly concerned with simple economic issues: specifically, guaranteed full employment and a steady rise in living standards."[5]

Raymond Williams, writing about Britain as that nation moves into the 1970s, notes the same characteristic in the general population and tries to account for its existence:

. . . there is a kind of stabilized poverty and neglect, and the creation of new forms of essentially orderly control and direction, toward narrowed social ends, with at the edge, and now quite virtuously displayed, the power of the state and the law ready to deal with protesting minorities. This is the order we are invited to celebrate, to make marginal choices inside. Its whole point is the distancing, the displacement and the manipulation of conflicts, and the direction of the society toward false definitions which are repeated so often as to seem the only condition of sanity. Any other possibilities not only seem, but in the short term are, impractical—so impractical that only the young can believe in them.[6]

We are rediscovering that the power to define reality and to set the social agenda for the community-at-large is the key to social control—a point noted by both Jerry Rubin, who writes that "The power to define is the power to control,"[7] and Senator Fulbright, who states that "communication is power, and exclusive access to it is a dangerous, unchecked power."[8] Definitional control in America has been held securely (at least until recently) by the controllers of the mass media and their ancillary services: PR, advertising, opinion polling, and the many paraeducational structures.

What people see and read and hear, what they wear, what they eat, where they go, and what they believe they are doing have become functions of an informational system that sets tastes and values according to its own self-reinforcing market criteria. In an earlier time, economic impoverishment established the criteria.

Daniel Bell calls knowledge "a strategic resource" and observes that "as with all resources, the question becomes, who will control it, who will make the necessary decisions about allocations?" He seeks a "balance of knowledge and power to spell out the technical components and the dimensions of cost; to widen the options and to specify the moral context of choices so that decisions may be made more consciously and with a greater awareness of responsibility."[9]

But, of course, it is the failure to achieve this condition that depresses so many. The ability to use knowledge morally and humanistically, so that all the consequences of decision-making are available for prior scrutiny, is precisely what the system of control in the advanced market-directed industrial state, especially so far as the mass media are concerned, does it best to curtail. It does so not because the decision-makers are deliberately malevolent, but because long-term social considerations are invariably at odds with short-term advantage, and a market economy is based on the immediate realization of self-interest.

The mechanics of the system-at-large, moreover, become deeply internalized in the values and thought processes of people who have been schooled early and repeatedly to translate their personal conditions into a national calculus of short-run payoffs. This is now recognized as the situation and mind set of so-called "middle America." It does not describe, however, the condition of some of the newer additions to, or trainees for, the knowledge labor force. This group, a numerous and growing contingent (the university student population alone is now more than half the size of the nation's corps of production workers in manufacturing), has begun to create a very different system of social measurement. So much so, in fact, that the issue that Drucker foresees as the problem of the future, the "manageability" of the knowledge worker/trainee, is already the crisis of the present.

Whatever the perspective, there is no denying that among the youth with above-average education and family income, a deeply felt hostility to the commercialized information–recreation society has emerged. William McGill, president of Columbia University, estimates that "anywhere from a third to a half of the students today fall into the alienated group."[10] A study transmitted to the President's Commission on Campus Unrest found that "almost all college students believe some form of confrontation 'is necessary and effective' in changing society," and that "three quarters of the students agreed with the statement that 'basically, the United States is a racist society.' "[11] Staughton Lynd sees it this way:

Education tries to shape the young for [this] unmanly and inhuman adult work-life, and so itself becomes a target. The rapid expansion of higher education since the end of World War II came about because of technological change in industry. Automatized and computerized industry require more and more young men and women who have white-collar skills but behave with the docility expected of blue-collar workers. The thrust of the multiversity in which so many of our 7 million college students are trained is toward skilled obedience. The student, like the worker he is intended to become, uses his mind as well as his hands, but not creatively, not at his own initiative, still within limits set by orders coming down from above. That is what modern higher education is like, too. And the students tell those who give them orders to practice being foremen on someone else. In their own minds, they refuse to be bent, folded, spindled, and mutilated.[12]

Labeling the repudiation of standard American values a "counter culture," Theodore Roszak[13] and others attribute this swelling youthful opposition to the rigidities and conformities imposed on society by technology. Roszak attacks the manipulative culture as the inevitable outgrowth of a rampaging technology. The specific social organization that determines the character of technology and its applications is regarded as irrelevant in this view. Ironically, the breakaway culture that Roszak supports is itself subject to the same distortions that "straight" society suffers from its absorption with technology. Youth's new life style has become a profitable activity. Rock festivals, record promotions, cult foods, and costumes become enterprise ventures for hip capitalists, and "liberation" itself becomes a salable commodity. The "movement" becomes the market. Apparently it is not technology alone, but certain types of criticism of industrialism as well, that succumb to a specific social system.

Still, the indigenous American "cultural revolution," with all its vulnerabilities and dependencies, undermines the traditional values of conventional society. Work, discipline, hierarchy, and repression are under continuous attack, and often the private enterprisers who use the new outlook and style for routine profit-making contribute to the unraveling of the social order and to the freeing of emotional currents whose direction no one can safely predict.

Automatic instrumentation, which may eventually dispense altogether with ordinary human labor, is imminent (in a historical sense at least), and awareness of the possibility of permanent escape from the traditional coercive nature of work has already permeated youthful consciousness. Since the underlying institutional arrangements give no sign of adapting to this entirely new technological capability, the conflict has broken out on the personal behavioral (cultural) level, concealing—and, for the time being, denying—the deeper economic–social issues that underlie cultural revolt.

In the sixties, the nation seemed to have "lost" its youth to a hedonistic nihilism with undertones of violence and irrationality. The scene in the early seventies is somewhat more quiet, but the lull may be misleading. In any case, it is the unyielding socioeconomic order, buffeted by an exploding technology yet resistant to structural change, that explains the wildly swinging compass of youth's emotion.

A growing number of knowledge workers/trainees are unable to accept the premises of the goods economy. Their schooling and their experience, limited as they may be, have raised doubts about a society that puts everything on sale and, despite its assertions to the contrary, values the human being only as an afterthought. Ironically, the mass media are the sources of this subversive revelation. The same media messages that produce, or at least reinforce, the thinking of the "hard-hats" also convince many youths, whose backgrounds permit them to sample more fully the offerings of the consumer society, of the vacuity and personal destructiveness of the system's values. The $23 billion annual private advertising budget has done an effective, if unintentional, job of awakening those whose perceptions have escaped total distortion at an early age to the true character of the American Way.

This, then, is the growing dilemma of media managers in the United States today. *Laissez faire* in media matters solidifies the age–income split in the nation and makes the knowledge trainees less and less "manageable." Interventionism brings with it uncertainty and the possibility of deeper, though latent, social conflicts. The increasingly tense social condition, however, precludes *laissez faire*. We are encountering, therefore, the first indications of deliberate governmental intervention in the national information process. Communications decisions are becoming more political and consequently less commercial, though, of course, this is still a very uneven process. The trend has been observed and reported optimistically, it seems, as a source of future commercial business. A McGraw-Hill Publishing Company functionary foresees, for instance, . . . that government, which has to govern more and more by voter consent, will come into communications in a big way, learn to speak the language of the people, and use advertising to sell its "product."[14]

For this to occur without creating widespread fear and anxiety in the nation requires, first of all, popular enlightenment on the derelictions of the commercial mass media. And this has been the special contribution of Vice-President Agnew and the tight ring of insiders making up President Nixon's White House staff. Their indictments of the media are introductory efforts to accustom the nation to overt governmental intervention in the informational process, because the commercial communications system cannot be trusted. Accordingly, we get a surprisingly frank, if only partly accurate, critique of the private media, which have hitherto had little difficulty passing as an objective recreational and news system. Now we are informed by the Vice-President that there is network control of news and programming, a situation in which *the news that 40 million Americans receive each night is determined by a handful of men responsible only to their corporate employers and is filtered through a handful of commentators who admit to their own set of biases. . . .* [*There is*] *a virtual monopoly of a whole medium of communications. . .* [*There is a*] *trend toward monopolization of the great public information vehicles* [*newspapers*] *and the concentration of more and more power in fewer and fewer hands . . .* [*And, consequently,*] *the time for naive belief in their press and network neutrality is gone.*[15]

Certainly, the picture is not overdrawn, although Vice-President Agnew, ignoring a very rich historical record of similar criticism from a different perspective, seems to feel that he is the first to have called attention to these conditions.[16]

If anything, the control of the nation's informational apparatus is even more tightly held than Agnew and his associates suggest. It is not only a matter of the influence of the *New York Times* and the *Washington Post*, important as those organs of opinion are. As far as the press is concerned, the lack of competing voices has now reached an almost unsurpassable point. One longtime observer of these matters writes,

Whereas in 1880 only 38% of U.S. cities were single daily cities, and only one city had a single-ownership combination, today 85.6% of the cities have only one daily. If the 150 cities with two dailies under a single ownership and the 21 cities with two dailies in joint-operating arrangements are added to the 1,284 single daily cities, the number of cities without commercially competing local dailies rises to 97% of the total. In only 45 of the 1,500 daily newspaper cities today are there two or more commercially competing dailies, and in only three of these 45 cities are there more than two ownerships of daily newspapers of general content and circulation.[17]

Broadcasting facilities are no less concentrated. Though there are over seven hundred commercial TV stations and more than

6,700 commercial radio stations in the country, control is heavily pyramided through chain ownerships, mixed media holdings (newspapers owning stations) and, most importantly, the funneling of most of television programming through three networks, with one or another of which nearly every local station is affiliated.[18] Furthermore, in television, the newest and most compelling communications medium, a narrow base of control has existed from the outset. Those who received the first licenses granted in 1951 by the Federal Communications Commission have remained at the center of the profit-making and have led the way in concentrating holdings.[19]

Normal market mechanics have produced an industrial structure in the mass media indistinguishable from that of other business sectors. Vice-President Agnew calls attention to this also: "Should a conglomerate be formed that tied together a shoe company with a shirt company, some voice will rise up righteously to say that this is a great danger to the economy and that the conglomerate ought to be broken up. But a single company, in the nation's capital, holds control of the largest newspaper in Washington, D.C., and one of the four major television stations, and an all-news radio station, and one of the three major national news magazines . . ."[20]

In brief, the mass media, and broadcasting in particular, are highly profitable commercial enterprises. Across the board, taking the high earners with the low, television is a vast money-making machine.[21]

High profitability and easy access to congressional favor give media owners a very privileged position in the economy. But even more significant is the indispensable support that the media provide to the commercial–financial system in general, reinforcing market objectives at every turn.

Why, then, should the vital informational apparatus of the managerial–industrial order be attacked by governmental leaders recruited from, and beholden to, corporate enterprise? Why can it not be relied upon to do what it always did well in the past—secure the firm attachment of its national audience to the *status quo*? Ordinary market mechanics offer a partial explanation.

Further reasons rest, it seems, on the rapidly shifting nature of the political–social climate in the United States. Consider first the commercial factor.

There is no disagreement on the enormous contributions the mass media make to the furtherance of American commodity production and distribution. TV moves goods best, according to Arthur Nielsen, founder of the well-known marketing research organization.[22] J. K. Galbraith also has observed that the industrial system would be a shambles without the consumer-goods image-creating machinery of the home screen.[23] A consequence of the total involvement of the popular informational–entertainment channels with marketing is that even news reports and informational programs are treated as commodities. Sir William Haley, former director–general of the British Broadcasting Corporation, put it this way: "Like so much else in American life today, it [the news] comes second to salesmanship. News, is in fact, being used as a kind of entertainment."[24]

Newscasters and commentators are first of all salesmen. Viewers are sought as competitively for the news as for any other program because commercials have to be sold to sustain the "show," and, more importantly, because viewers lost at 6 P.M. to a rival newscaster may be lost for the high-priced prime-time hours of subsequent programming as well. So news operates under the same commercial imperatives as the rest of the schedule. The result, inevitably, is a continuing frenetic search by the programmers for excitement, sensation, and action in reportage. What affords more opportunity than the most cataclysmic daily events of this era? Furthermore, the social order appears to be coming apart at the seams, as both new and generations-old troubles accumulate, surface, and press for resolution. Urban decay, crime, racism, environmental pollution, and war are the everyday conditions of life for tens of millions of people.* The mass media

* The Sixth Annual International Security Conference, a commercial fair exhibiting surveillance, alarm, detection, and security devices for all tastes and situations, is an interesting reflection of the current social condition in the United States. See "The Paranoia Market" by John Stickney, *Harper's* (September, 1972), pp. 34–39.

journeyman would have to be incredibly inept to overlook entirely such powerful raw material of social upheaval.

The actual conditions of society and the commercial motivation to attract and hold an audience combine to provide the nightly viewer–listener with at least some glimmering of a disintegrating *status quo*. The picture, obviously, is not pretty. Hence the rising clamor, from a multiplying host of adherents to the way things used to be, to stop "manufacturing" or "distorting" reality. This is the backdrop to the storm of conservative outrage against the televised violence of the Chicago police at the Democratic National Convention in the summer of 1968.

What is occurring now is the open repudiation not only of the hallowed principle of full news coverage, which has rarely, if ever, been seriously implemented in the media, but also of the commercial rule of keeping the level of excitement sufficiently high to attract an audience. Spiro Agnew admonishes: ". . . And in the networks' endless pursuit of controversy, we should ask: What is the end value—to enlighten or *to profit?* (emphasis mine) What is the end result—to inform or to confuse? How does the ongoing exploration for more action, more excitement, more drama serve our national search for internal peace and stability?"[25] Apparently the threat to the social order is sufficiently grave, in this Administration's view, to call into question what the nation has always prized most, the quest for profitability.

But failing far-reaching structural change, it is traditional *status quo* behavior to conceal if possible, cosmeticize if necessary, and, in any case, minimize, the extent of the social disarray. In this period of communications saturation—almost every American home possesses at least one radio and television set, and some have two and three of each—this requires, to be even minimally effective, massive control and manipulation. It is just such an effort that recent governmental statements and actions herald. Actually, the process predates the intervention of the White House, and has been well under way for several years.

Generally speaking, the condition of the information system has invariably been commercial, self-selective, and, in the main, reactionary. Furthermore, this was achieved very effectively without central direction, by structures that operated within implicit generalized assumptions common to all property-holders, media-controllers certainly not excepted. What is different now is not only a matter of degree, but also of the introduction of explicit manipulatory methods.

Consider, for instance, radio–television's performance after Martin Luther King's murder. As the industry's trade magazine described it, "Television and radio emerged with new esteem last week from what may have been the stormiest ten days of news coverage in their history." What merited this self-congratulation? In the words of *Broadcasting*, again, "a spot survey of some stations in several of the major markets where civil disorders occurred showed that at the local level the theme was 'restraint.'" And how was this "restraint" exercised in practice? In Baltimore, for instance, a news director said, "films of police firing on snipers, white men with guns in the trouble area and black militants were reported but not generally as voiced by them."[26] Television in some cities ran movies day and night. And *Variety* reported with some astonishment how many black faces were seen on the home screen for one week after King's death, only to vanish once the passions subsided.

The media, largely abandoning their never widely fulfilled function as informational sources, were used deliberately for diversion, sedation, and pacification.

In Washington, D.C., officials turned to a 34-year-old Negro singer whose ability to work up an audience had long been established. Before TV *cameras and radio microphones, James Brown poured his soul into a message urging an end to the disorders in the city . . . "Go home, look at* TV. *Listen to the radio. Listen to some James Brown records."*[27]

Still more significantly, voluntary agreements among broadcasters to suppress news on racial troubles, as well as compacts with police agencies to delay or even withhold information on urban disorders, are multiplying. A survey conducted by one media journal disclosed that:

about one quarter of all stations [TV] subscribe to some kind of such agreement. The larger stations (those with $3 million or more in annual revenue) reported the largest number of such compacts, which is not surprising considering the prevalence of disorders in the large cities. Nearly 39 percent of large station respondents reported operating under some kind of pact or informal agreement.[28]

An example of a tie-in between broadcasters and police is also reported:

Stations in Indianapolis follow the "Omaha Plan" which provides that when a "Code 30" is announced by police, news media agree to withhold the release of the story for 30 minutes but can continue to cover it for information. WFBM-TV *said that successive Code 30s can be called by police but* WISH-TV *understands the agreement to mean that only a second 30-minute blackout can be called by police after which each station is free to cover the story.*

Some agreements go so far as to ban broadcast news while a disorder is in progress. Others require media not to mention the location of the disturbance. Memphis is an example of the latter.[29]

Coordinated news control is being institutionalized on a private, as well as governmental, basis. Expecting a troubled fall in 1970, the National Association of Broadcasters in "an unprecedented call" advised its members "to be especially careful in their news coverage" of desegregation and campus unrest. The recommendation of news management was expressed in reassuring language:

It is not the purpose of the NAB *to intrude into the processes of news gathering and responsible reporting or the full flow of freedom that must underpin all of our industry's information efforts. Rather, we would sound the alert before the fact to urge you to anticipate any eventuality that might arise. We hope with you that reason and domestic tranquility prevail, but if they do not, we must be ready. Broadcast journalism is now the cornerstone of our broad service to the public and our responsibilities are therefore of the highest order as we present the news of the day.*[30]

Contrary to Vice-President Agnew's argument that the media have given protesters disproportionate coverage, there has been a calculated effort at the highest level of policy-making to mute criticism, and, wherever possible, to ignore it, even when the numbers and personalities at the rallies made them major newsworthy events by any professional criteria of measurement. *Variety* reported that "the massive Washington, D.C. and San Francisco anti-war marches and rallies [November 15, 1969] received no live or special coverage from the networks." The paper observed that "one objective of Veepee Spiro T. Agnew's high-voltage blast at network news operations last week was to squelch, if possible, any extensive moratorium coverage. He needn't have bothered."[31] The networks had had no intention of covering the gatherings live. But this was not a new development. *Variety* interviewed a network spokesman who recalled a

similar situation with the 1967 Pentagon March when the Johnson Administration was appeased without public outburst. NBC *News was definitely planning live coverage of the march when* CBS *News presented the proposition that they all eschew live coverage.* NBC *went along. Also contacted was* ABC, *and there was a coverage blackout of an event which was at least newsworthy enough to win Norman Mailer a Pulitzer prize for his book about it.*

The situation is deteriorating rapidly, and the *Variety* reporter concluded that

. . . there are a complexity of factors working against network news before a high government official comes along to bully them via their own facilities. Generally conservative and profit-oriented network managements have no sympathy for extra and controversial coverage. Even more conservative affiliates can be down-

right hostile to issue-oriented TV *reportage. Tough newsmen have been weeded out of the network news departments over the last few years. And then there was the public uproar when the Chicago Convention's chaotic reality ran contrary to network* TV*'s constantly grinding fantasies about such things as law and order.*[32]

The process of intimidation, quietly applied, was explained to one reporter by a CBS producer:

This Administration has two techniques for manipulating the networks. One is the "early warning letter" addressed to Frank Stanton, say, from Herb Klein. It says something like, "We understand you are planning a program or feature on nuclear carriers or some such topic. We trust you will be checking with so-and-so at the Pentagon to get all the facts you need . . ."

Dr. Stanton sends the letter on to Dick Jencks, who sends it over to Dick Salant, who sends it down the hall to the vice president for news or specials, who sends it to the executive producer, who sends it to the producer . . . Each executive scribbles on the buck slip "What's up?" or "What's this about?"—and promptly puts the matter out of his mind. After all, he's asked someone else to look into it. The guy at the end of the line is naturally all shook up. He's the lowest man on the totem pole and knows if he goes ahead with the project and there's a complaint, he is the one in trouble since everyone else has, in effect, called it to his attention. So you damn well call so-and-so at the Pentagon and wrap your item in a lot of bland cotton . . . The second technique is the "eleventh-hour telegram." Again, it goes right to Stanton. It may come from a Cabinet officer, and it warns of "the great danger in putting out a biased account" unless an interview with so-and-so is included. This last-minute appeal is intended to shake them up so much that the project doesn't get on the air . . . I've seen it happen.[33]

Examples of the media's voluntary knuckling-under to pressure are too numerous to detail. A few of the more egregious instances in recent years include Ralph Nader's tabooed appearance on Johnny Carson's "Tonight" show;[34] the ban on a satirical album, "The Begatting of the President," on several commercial stations;[35] Lawrence Ferlinghetti's "Tyrannus Nix," taped by the poet for National Educational Television and sharply trimmed by NET without Ferlinghetti's knowledge or permission;[36] a special presidential briefing for top executives and editors of thirty-eight selected television and newspaper organizations, to which the *New York Times* and the *Washington Post*, both outspoken critics of the Administration's Cambodia venture and general Indochina policy, were not invited;[37] and American Broadcasting Company's cancellation of an appearance by Angela Davis on the Dick Cavett show, after her acquittal, because the show lacked "balance."[38]

The deteriorating national informational condition goes well beyond individual episodic censorship by high bureaucrats. Executive manipulation of the media, limned brilliantly by Joe McGinnis in *The Selling of the President, 1968*, has developed into a fine art. Nowhere else is the ideational environment so effectively packaged as at the national level. The *New York Times*, singled out for attack by the Nixon Administration, reported some of the techniques utilized to create a controlled informational perspective. It described top-level briefings of news executives, designed to bypass the less cooperative Washington press corps; personal presidential visits to especially receptive newspaper editors; packaged press releases nationally distributed to 1,200 editorial writers and radio and television news directors; and, most important of all until even they began to disappear, the elaborately arranged and nationally televised presidential press conferences. The *Times* noted that "he [Nixon] selects the reporters who will ask the questions. As every President has, Mr. Nixon has questions he wants to answer planted in the press. Moreover, few reporters, knowing the camera is on them, have shown themselves adept at asking sharp questions."[39]

Presidential public relations also are applied to the media journeymen. Mike Royko, a Chicago-based columnist, wondered first why he was asked to a Presidential social event, and then about the purpose of his five-minute chat with the President on the receiving line. He mused:

And the President, was there, straining his mind and using time, in the capacity of a salesman, or a public relations man. Through a handshake and an exchange of pleasantries, we were all to go away thinking more highly of his foreign policies . . . That's what I mean about it being a strange way to run a country. . . . I think he ought to forget about selling and just demonstrate that the product works.[40]

There is now also the staged event—an important means of attracting the nation's attention and then of organizing its consciousness. Though not the first chief executive to rely on this technique, President Nixon has used it to advantage on several occasions. Illustrative is the style of his return from China in early 1972. On the flight home, his airplane was kept on the ground for several hours in Newfoundland to permit his arrival in the United States to be synchronized with peak television-viewing hours. This tactic was repeated on a still more heroic scale on the President's return from Moscow in May, 1972. The final hop of that flight was made by helicopter from a Washington airport to the steps of the Capitol. There, before the unseen prime-time television audience, the President's party alighted from the plane, marched up the steps of the Capitol, and made a triumphal entry before a joint session of Congress, convened apparently as a backdrop for presidential publicity.

Again, the mounting of the Republican National Convention in Miami in August, 1972, was more like a theatrical event than an important exercise in a democratic selection process. Here is one reporter's account:

Everything that went into the three-day convention program—even the opening and closing prayers—had to be submitted for approval and inclusion in a prepared script.

The script, detailed down to instructions to speakers like actor John Wayne to "accept cheers and applause," and to retired football star Bart Starr to "nod" to students presenting the colors . . .

The elaborate script was in development over 2½ months' time.[41]

The staged event is not the exclusive domain of the nation's political leaders. It is in vogue across the country. Much attention has been paid to the relatively few instances when it has been appropriated by the youth movement. Yet such efforts are entirely dependent on the willingness of the controllers of the media to play along. Sometimes they do. More often they do not. The unreliability of access to the media is no problem, however, for the well-established forces of the social order. As long as the sponsors of an event have credentials certified as legitimate, widespread publicity is usually assured.

The huge TV audiences for professional football, for example, provide a weekly opportunity, during the several-month season, for massive doses of nationalism and militarism. All sorts of inspirational messages are carefully imbedded in the "recreational" interludes staged during the half-time intervals. Most of the time the sponsorship is unmentioned, if not unknown. In two instances—a tribute to American prisoners-of-war at the Army–Navy football game in the fall of 1970 and the choice of an escaped POW to throw out the first ball to open the professional baseball season in 1971—it was revealed that the public relations were organized by the Nixon Administration.[42]

Still another instrument of the developing public-opinion manipulation is the omnipresent poll. Opinion surveys are employed increasingly to create the atmosphere sought by the information managers at the highest level. The origin of, and support for, most of the surveys is generally obscure, though the most prestigious names in public-opinion sounding are employed. No one can estimate the full extent to which independent survey firms are enlisted by the government for the latter's purposes, but the following passage from a USIA-produced film, *The Silent Majority*, is suggestive of the ties that now exist:

Correspondent: *For the last 33 years the American Institute of Public Opinion has been a respected reporter of American attitudes. The Institute—known as the Gallup Poll—has pioneered techniques of public sampling, and has refined the methods of research which are used all over this country and by foreign opinion research organizations in all parts of the world . . . George Gallup is president of the Gallup Poll organization. Today, we'd like to question him about one of his most recent polls. . . . On November 3rd* [1969] *President Nixon spoke to the people of the United States about his policy on Vietnam. He mentioned a "silent majority" of Americans who, he felt, supported his position. What did your organization do following that speech?*

Mr. Gallup: *Well, immediately following the speech we had a squad of well-trained telephone interviewers contact 500 people across the country and then the results came in the same night, of course, and we collected them the next day and wired the results off to our newspapers at one o'clock on Tuesday.*[43]

The close association of the Gallup Poll with the presidential message, and the official (and rapid) distribution overseas by the USIA of the poll's results and Gallup's comments, indicate a relationship which can hardly instill confidence about the independence of the information-producing and opinion-polling process.

Domestically, the connections between governmental authorities and polling companies are a totally uncharted area, but one whose usefulness for manipulation can hardly be overstated.

Even when the polls are not being utilized for deliberate mind management, they may nonetheless have that effect. Joseph Klapper, director of social research for the Columbia Broadcasting System, observes that:

. . . there is another area in which mass communication is extremely effective, and that is in the creation of opinion on new issues. By "new issues" I mean issues on which the individual has no opinion and on which his friends and fellow group members have no opinion. The reason for the effectiveness of mass com-

> *munications in creating opinions on new issues is pretty obvious:* The individual has no predisposition to defend, and so the communication falls, as it were, on defenseless soil. *And once the opinion is created, then it is this new opinion which becomes easy to reinforce and hard to change. This process of opinion creation is strongest, by the way, when the person has no other source of information on the topic to use as a touchstone. He is therefore, the more wholly dependent on the communication in question* (emphasis mine).[44]

Questions that in themselves are value judgments, or biased perspectives, create an attitudinal framework into which the respondent is pressed by his very participation in the process. More significantly, the impact goes well beyond the poll participant. The nation-at-large is influenced when the poll is published or broadcast.

Much the same conclusion is reached by another writer who notes that:

> *we must realize that preferences reported in sample surveys, electronic or otherwise, are often very different in nature than those actively volunteered when citizens participate. The opinions expressed in polls are frequently shallow responses to problems to which the respondent has never given much thought. The saliency of the issue to him may be low and the opinion is likely to be based on little or no information.*[45]

The passive polling process, therefore, is apt to be an instrument for opinion creation, not only for the directly participating respondents but, more significantly, for the millions who learn from polls what national sentiment is supposed to be on such questions.

The controlled domestic informational environment has its international counterpart in the expanding communications activities of governmental agencies, the USIA in particular. Still, it is important to remember that mind management begins at home, and that the United States public is the first beneficiary/victim of controlled information. The current scale of such operations is discernible in the preparation of the public for foreign military interventions or new departures in foreign policies, such as the formulation of the Truman Doctrine in 1947 and the Vietnamese intervention in the mid-1960s.

Richard M. Freeland offers a "revised" interpretation of the origins of McCarthyism. He traces it to some of the methods employed by President Truman and his closest advisors in the immediate post-World War II period. Freeland quotes a memorandum from Assistant Secretary of State Will Clayton, dated March 5, 1947, which proposed that Congress appropriate five billion dollars for foreign aid. Clayton wrote, "the United States will not take world leadership effectively unless the people of the United States are shocked into doing so." He recommended "an exposé of the communist threat as the proper means of achieving this."[46]

Howard K. Smith, the news commentator, gave a congressional hearing a similar account.

Mr. Smith: *Senator Vandenberg suggested to President Truman if he wanted to take such a drastic step as commit America to the defense of Greece and Turkey, "If that is what you want to do, Mr. President, you had better go before Congress and scare the hell out of the American people," and Truman did it.*

[Congressman] Fascell: *He scared Congress, too.*

Mr. Smith: *In July 1965, when the decision was made to go into Vietnam in force, it was discussed at great length in Cabinet meetings, and in National Security Council meetings and smaller meetings, whether or not to try to scare hell out of the people, and the decision was deliberate not to do so.*[47]

Whichever way decision-makers move in any particular situation, the central and unprecedented fact is that information control has become part of national policy. The techniques of ideational packaging have become instruments for manipulating popular support for (or, at least, indifference to) governmental actions.

This may help to explain the seemingly paradoxical condition that no other nation (with the possible exception of some Western European countries) approaches American gross informational levels, as measured by radio and television set ownership and use, and yet, according to Senator Stuart Symington, ". . . the public in this country often knows less than much of the rest of the world."[48]

In fact, it cannot be emphasized too strongly that there appears to be a new direction in domestic informational activities. The communications editor of the *Saturday Review* refers to a "Coming Age of News Monopoly" and writes that "we feel we must at the very least put up storm-warning flags before the hurricane of fascism, monopoly, one-man rule, and press gag engulfs our democracy."[49] Unreservedly commercial in the past, and assuming a matter-of-fact support of the social–industrial order as the natural consequence of their activities, the media and ancillary informational services today are being pushed, and are moving independently, onto a directly manipulative path. The growth of a large knowledge industry work force suggests to the country's media managers the necessity for ever-widening control of the informational and cultural environment. At the same time, increasingly explosive social and political issues create a daily atmosphere of crisis, and if the media even dimly reflect this reality, passions are further enflamed and powerful custodians of the *status quo*, including the President, are aroused to fury and intimidation. The efforts to suppress the publication of the Pentagon Papers are striking evidence of these tendencies.

Accordingly, a deliberate effort is developing, at influential levels of government, to move beyond manipulation to restrict, censor, and anesthetize the most widely used communications channels. Clay T. Whitehead, the Director of the Office of Telecommunications Policy and "White House Broadcasting Czar,"[50] immediately after President Nixon's re-election proposed that local broadcasters, a notoriously conservative breed, monitor and, when necessary, reject network news, documentary, and entertainment programs if they included, in Whitehead's open-ended phrase, "ideological plugola."

Fred Friendly, one-time president of CBS News, termed this proposal "the most dangerous thing to come along in 50 years of broadcasting."[51] The *New York Times* editorialized: "The White House message to American broadcasters—commercial, public and educational—is coming through louder and clearer every day. That message is blunt: Stay away from controversial subjects . . . The voices of Congress and the public will have to be heard if broadcasting is not to be turned into a counterpart of the domestic United States Information Agency."[52]

More ominous still, the *New York Times* reported almost matter-of-factly in the Fall of 1970 that the President had already appointed "the nation's chief censor, a private citizen now on standby duty who would assume office in a national emergency." A "little-known" plan, which has been in existence, according to the *Times*, for several years, permits the President to decree a national emergency without congressional approval and to institute press censorship.[53]

Actually, the chief censor had not been appointed, but all the arrangements governing the installation of wartime censorship —now termed "wartime informational security"[54]—in case there occurs a vaguely defined national emergency, are drafted.

Representative William S. Moorhead, the chairman of the Congressional Subcommittee on U.S. Government Information Policies and Practices, has voiced his alarm over the direction and tempo of these executive branch activities. He told Congress in October, 1972:

. . . *As I looked behind the sworn testimony of* OEP [Office of Emergency Preparedness] *witnesses who implied that their censorship and information-collection plan would be put into effect only if there were a nuclear attack on the United States, I found they are ready to impose censorship in the United States when we become involved in a foreign conflict just like the Vietnam War. . . .*

Section 1 of chapter 4 of the national censorship plan explains the contingencies under which the censorship system will be activated:

The contingencies to be considered in any emergency planning within the Federal Government are many and varied. In planning for National Censorship it is necessary to consider only those contingencies or situations wherein the National Security may require imposition of such censorship. Generally stated these are: (a) General War; (b) Limited war, or conflicts of the "brush fire" type, in which United States forces are involved elsewhere in the world on land, sea, or in the air.

The Government's official plan permits censorship not only in a general, nuclear war but also in a limited conflict the President might involve us in anywhere in the world. And some of the details of this censorship plan were apparently worked out by a political security operative who was caught spying for the Republican Party on the inner workings of the Democratic Party.[55]

It is still too early to predict whether these proliferating efforts will succeed. Some countervailing forces are also operative. Concentrated as the main sources of information are, alternative channels, far weaker and with much narrower constituencies, do exist. Unfortunately, most of these channels are reaching only a very limited stratum of the population—the young, university graduates, and, for the most part, the well-to-do. The split in the national community is deepening, therefore, along informational —as well as generational, professional, racial, and political—lines.

CHAPTER EIGHT

Information Technology as a Democratizing Force?

> *. . . the hard facts of history support a gloomy but realistic prognostication. The economics of commercial communications, as now organized and financed, will almost inevitably dim, if not extinguish, many of the bright hopes of this fourth and potentially greatest generation of electronic media . . .*
>
> STANLEY SCOTT
> "Lessons from the History of American Broadcasting," *Science*
> 22 December 1972, p. 1264

THE CONDITIONS UNDER WHICH information is purveyed in America today are controlled by concentrated private economic power. Press and broadcasting chains interlock with "knowledge" conglomerates. Lubricating and underwriting these essentially private communications complexes, which provide the substantive content of the country's formal and para-educational–learning outputs, are the advertising expenditures of the nation's supercorporations. Separate from, but by no means independent of, these power groupings is the national governmental bureaucracy, which generates a mass of data, much of which never reaches the public.

It is in this context that the United States finds itself entering still another "new era"—the era of so-called information abundance. It was, after all, only in 1965 that Harold Lasswell, a veteran social analyst, considered the "policy problems of a data-rich society."[1]

One astounding discovery in communications has succeeded another. The past few years have witnessed the development of TV, satellite communications, the computer, cable TV, TV cassettes, and the ultimate "information utility"—the linkage of computer to home terminals via cable TV. Understandably, the new techniques have aroused considerable enthusiasm, and not a few uncritical prophecies of vast social benefits. Not the least of the attractions for a market society of the production of new hardware is the profits it provides. But more important still, at least at this stage of national disorientation, is the revitalization of the myth of uninterrupted *technological progress*. The new instrumentation, we are told, will simultaneously provide quantity, quality, and instantaneity of information. All the promise and excitement that accompanied the communications innovations of the past are revived. Communications satellites, it is said, will draw us closer to distant nations, as the transoceanic cables failed to do, and thereby reduce suspicions and hostilities. Satellites, we are told, will offer poor and deprived nations the opportunity to leapfrog into the present, and will facilitate vast educational programs via direct TV broadcasting to their illiterate peoples.

As might be predicted, the main benefits of the new technology are expected to accrue to our own already-privileged population. Indicative of the euphoric mood is this appraisal:

Although this first stage of the new media era will cause dislocations in existing media, it will also open up enough new channels of mass communication to evaporate the twentieth century threat of press monopoly. With so many channels available to all the pluralistic views and tastes of society, the free [sic] *countries will have a new opportunity to establish a "libertarian" press system. Authoritarian societies, of course, will use this new technology as just another tool in their arsenals of control.*[2]

There are similarly optimistic, if more guarded, predictions that the home-based "information utility" will foster full public participation in the decision-making processes of government.[3] Some of the technical requirements for organizing such a participatory system are examined in the *Minerva* research project of the Center for Policy Research.[4] In brief, the proposals describe the technical potential for developing a two-way communications flow between transmitter and receiver, based on a greater channel capacity. (Cable TV already provides forty channels, and many more are considered feasible as the technology is improved.) Less attention is paid to the possibility of establishing crude stimulus–response types of circuits, but we will return to this subject later.

Exuberant expectations for technological solutions to social crises are an old story in the United States. Surveying the past in an essay aptly titled "The History of the Future," two writers note that the ideology of the technologically oriented futurists "can serve as a form . . . of 'false consciousness,' a deflection away from the substantial problems of the present." They continue: "Despite the manifest failure of technology to resolve pressing social issues over the last century, contemporary intellectuals continue to see revolutionary potential in the latest technological gadgets which are pictured as a force *outside* history and politics." They conclude: "the 'third communications revolution' has within it the same seeds of miscarriage that have historically attended innovations in communications. Rather than creating a 'new future,' modern technology invites the public to participate in a ritual of control where fascination with technology masks the underlying factors of politics and power."[5]

The suggestion that the data-rich society and its supportive hardware will dissolve our current social ills is both cruel and deceitful. It is cruel to suggest that ghetto children confronting computer consoles will magically overcome generations of deprivation. It is deceitful to allow preoccupation with electronic technology and technique to obscure the institutional underpinnings that continue to be responsible for the direction and focus of the new instrumentation.

The central questions concerning the character of, and prospects for, the new information technology are our familiar criteria: *for whose benefit and under whose control will it be implemented?* Much of the powerful instrumentation has originated, as we have observed, with the armed forces, in their assigned task of defending and extending the American corporate empire globally. Harold Sackman touches on this phenomenon briefly in his review of what he terms "the humanistic crisis in computer-serviced societies." "The main theme that runs through [Sackman's] account of the internal development of man–computer communication in the computer world . . . is that the public interest continues to be the last, not the first consideration, and that the individual user is still the forgotten man." He finds it "ironic that the first experimental time-sharing systems were also sponsored by public funds from the Department of Defense which enabled commercial firms to leapfrog over and profit from the worst and most expensive mistakes that are eventually committed in pioneering ventures." Sackman concludes that "the social stakes are too high to let the information revolution pass as just another economic opportunity to be resolved by the vagaries of the marketplace."[6]

Yet it is neither "ironic" nor accidental that military and private commercial interests have dominated the development of the new information technology. It is entirely in accord with the processes and mechanics of the concentrated private economic structure that now presides over American resource decisions. Departures from this pattern would be a genuine cause for wonderment. What Sackman's concerns do emphasize is the extent to which the "data-rich" society has already been enfolded in the institutional grip that its predecessor, the information-poor society, struggled against.

Cable TV, still in its infancy, is traveling the same free-enterprise path that led radio and television to their present lamentable condition. *Variety* reports that "the Cable Industry is going to be no less capitalistic and competitive than radio and television."[7]

In the absence of national policies, *ad hoc* local municipal arrangements for regulating the introduction of the many-channeled system are simply inadequate to defend the public interest and the educational–cultural needs of the people. Besides, the older monopolistic broadcasting giants are doing everything in their ample power to thwart the development of what they regard as a threat to their revenue-producing opportunities. Ralph Lee Smith, author of *The Wired Nation,* concludes that "faced with a new technology, our institutions seem incapable of implementing any concept of the public interest other than the accommodation of economic interests." Therefore, "the numerous services that broad-band (cable) systems can bring to city governments, to city school systems, and to poor and disadvantaged populations of our inner cities, the contributions that they can make to a revived sense of community through the creation of local and community broadcasting services, and the role that they can play in alleviating the profound feeling of voicelessness, through abundant channels and open access for the presentation of all views—these are sacrificed in order that the economic interests of small, powerful groups will not be disturbed."[8]

Not only is the informational circuitry still firmly in corporate hands, but the data essential to prying open the closed system of privilege remain inaccessible. Basic information regarding the ownership of corporations (camouflaging stockholders' identities), the quality of the product ("trade secrets"), corporate profit statistics detailed by taxable assets, and cost and pricing data are practically undiscoverable, except in isolated and fragmentary cases.

It is still a gigantic task to secure *any* meaningful information, governmental or private, that reveals where control of the economy is actually vested. United States Senator Lee Metcalf, testifying before the Subcommittee on Monopoly of the Senate Small Business Committee, observed that "collection of data on financial concentration is so inadequate that the Government becomes ludicrous in its feeble efforts to determine facts and enforce laws and regulations. Last month, for example [May 1972], when the Federal Communications Commission liberalized its rules on bank ownership of broadcast companies, it admitted that banks were violating the old rules, and that the Commission did not know the extent of violations because it did not have current data . . ." Metcalf noted also that earlier in 1972 he had discovered that the Securities and Exchange Commission "could not provide a list of the thirty top stockholders of several major industrial corporations."[9]

The extent to which the government accedes to the corporate power structure's determination to withhold information is further revealed by Senator Gaylord Nelson, the Chairman of the Subcommittee on Monopoly of the Senate Small Business Committee, in a letter to the *Washington Post:*

. . . government secrecy supports corporate secrecy. Here is an example. The giant corporations have succeeded in erecting and fortifying in this country a public policy that equates not only apples and oranges but planets and oranges. In this incredible but real and present policy, the separate investments and profits made in any one of a global conglomerate's multi-million-dollar product lines are likened in all respects to the separate investment and profits made in a corner drugstore's soda fountain: both are protected as "proprietary data." Further, by building and perpetuating a myth that any politician calling for public disclosure of the conglomerate's product-line data would also want the drugstore's, big business has enlisted many small businessmen as allies in defense of an undiscriminating, codified policy of "business privacy." The alliance keeps most politicians tactfully quiet and the policy intact. Knowledge essential to either effective competition or effective regulation is thereby roped off as the statutory monopoly of a few corporate and governmental "big brothers."

Roll call votes in the Senate and House during last fall's [1971] debates on bills to extend wage and price control legislation are but the most recent evidence of this national policy's continued —and deeply regrettable—strength.

The bills requested by the administration and reported by both the Senate and House banking committees all contained similar sections making it a criminal offense for federal personnel receiving business information in connection with the economic stabilization program to disclose it to the public. The effect is to prevent both the public and Congress from monitoring the reasoning of the Price Commission, for example, in its evaluation of data received from the huge companies (*annual sales of $50 million or more*) *that must file reports either after or before they raise prices.*[10]

Corporate secrecy is further defended by business pressure groups which carry weight with the federal bureaucracy. One such association is the Business Advisory Council on Federal Reports, a group, according to Thomas De Baggio, "of big business executives who counsel the White House Office of Management and Budget (OMB) and through subgroups stall government requests for information."[11] Since the OMB has overall authority to sanction other governmental agencies' questionnaires, the Business Advisory Council's interventions may exercise incalculable influence over the collection or noncollection of data.

This is, of course, an example of the old-style way of exerting influence, and though it still probably represents the dominant method of exercising informational control, it is practically anachronistic. A pressure group of corporate leaders, no matter how prudent their contacts and associations, is occasionally discernible and certainly identifiable as a vehicle of manipulation when and if it is called to the attention of concerned parties.

The informational system now being created eliminates the individual and makes the process impersonal. This is not necessarily done out of an impulse to manipulate and conceal, but because it is efficient, available, and useful to those who currently make decisions. Hence, it presents altogether new problems for understanding the locus of control.

Definitional control—the power to set the rules of the game, the scope of the contest, and the limits of the challenge—is being *built into* the new information technology by interests that are certainly not coincidental with authentic national or social needs. *This need not occur*, but the prevailing distribution of power in society makes it almost inevitable that it will. The process by which the pattern unfolds has been described thus:

Power in the design of a large-scale computer-based system resides to an increasing degree with (1) the customer—to the extent that he can specify in complete and rigorous detail exactly what decisions he wishes to see implemented by his bureaucracy under every conceivable set of conditions, or (2) the system designer and computer programmer, who insure that some decision is made in every case whether that case has been clearly anticipated or not, and (3) the hardware manufacturers, whose technology and components determine what kind of data can be sensed and processed by computers, display equipment, and other system equipment.[12]

That a certain determinism will arise in this sequence of decisions is apparent. The customer, for no other reason than economics, has to be a large-scale corporation, a major governmental administrative unit, or, perhaps, a well-supported university. The programmers and designers are essentially technocrats, interested in the social process only insofar as it is reducible, *in its present state*, to their technical parameters. The hardware manufacturers are the electronic supergiants, which are certainly not pressing to design information systems that might challenge their dominance.

Though still in the formative stage, historically speaking, the character of the information technology seems already to have been cast in a rigid mold. A business study reports:

To date most of the information technology has been developed for solution of problems within a hierarchically-based institution such as the Department of Defense, NASA, *and the Atomic Energy Commission. . . . It is not too difficult to see that continued development of such information technology could well lead to establishing a mode of organizational structure based on the underlying mode of highly structured operations. This type of concept pervades the projected management styles for almost any of our institutions, i.e., national data banks,* EDUCOM, *and national computer centers are all oriented towards rigidly hierarchical organization forms.*[13]

Though the deep longing of many for community involvement and individual participation has been expressed with enormous poignancy time and time again in recent years, the new hardware systems are fostering still more inaccessible "top-down" informational channels. It is difficult to disagree with Robert Boguslaw's conclusion:

. . . whether the "masses" are denied legitimate access to decision makers by reason of despotism, bureaucratic deviousness, or simple technical obfuscation, the resultant erosion of democratic process can be much the same. To the extent that decisions made by equipment manufacturers, computer programmers, or system designers are enshrouded in the mystery of "technical" detail, the persons most affected by these decisions (including customers, publics, and employees) will be denied the opportunity to participate or react to the decision made. The spectrum of values represented in the new decision-making order can and is being increasingly circumscribed by fiat disguised as technological necessity. The paramount issues to be raised in connection with the design of our new computerized utopias are not technological—they are issues of values and the power through which these values become translated into action.[14]

It is important to emphasize that it is not the unavailability of "facts" that makes these developments so menacing. Facts by the billions will be supplied eagerly by increasingly capacious computers. It is the framework within which these "facts" are made available that is at issue. Who has asked the questions to which these "facts" are directed? Are these the questions that need to be answered, or should they even be raised? James Carey and John Quirk explain this well:

When one speaks, let us say, of the monopoly of religious knowledge, of the institutional church, one is not referring to the control of particles of information. Rather, one is referring to control of the entire system of thought, or paradigm, that determines what it is that can be religiously factual, that determines what the standards are for assessing the truth of any elucidation of these facts, that defines what it is that can be accounted for as knowledge. Modern computer enthusiasts may be willing to share their data with anybody. What they are not willing to relinquish as readily is the entire technocratic world-view that determines what it is that qualifies as an acceptable or valuable fact. What they monopolize is not the data itself but the approved, certified, sanctioned official mode of thought, indeed the definition of what it means to be reasonable.[15]

Who, then, can make the critical assessments that might stipulate a different set of capabilities for the new technology? Where may we look for independent assessment and evaluation, as well as technical expertise? This is the problem at the most elemental level. Edwin Parker of Stanford writes, "Given the greater economic incentives, vested interests, and institutional power that will accrue to the developers of the [new] technology relative to the assessors, it would be surprising if the weaker institution prevailed over the stronger." In short, the independent assessors are outside of the decisionmaking process. Decisions will be made regardless of their critiques. This observation leads Parker to advocate institutional assessment rather than technology assessment, although the same dilemma prevails. "If the institutions being assessed are dominant institutions in the society, then how can the inevitably weaker institution charged with responsibility for assessment muster enough economic and political power to effect changes?"[16]

Parker, along with the rest of us, cannot advance very far beyond this point, but his insistence that attention should be focused "at the place where the problems reside—in the basic institutional structure of the society," represents a refreshing recognition that information technology alone solves none of the social problems of the age, and may very well contribute to them.

Yet for the technologist, every problem has a technical solution. An issue such as hierarchical structure versus popular participation is, from this perspective, hardly an obstacle. The information–utility—the combination of computer and cable TV—is the latest in ultimate solutions. Its advocates claim that it can produce participatory programming, which permits the viewer/

receiver to react to and, some claim, to reformulate the context in which he is informationally engaged. Most of the discussion of this phenomenon centers on so-called mass polling and voting arrangements. In these situations, the home viewer may register choices or reactions to information delivered by means of a two-way circuit made available with broadband (cable) transmission.

Does this already-developed instrumentation offer even a modest prospect of achieving genuine popular participation? Will instantaneous voting and frequent polling overcome the atrophy which has seized the democratic process in the United States? Once more, the criteria that have been applied throughout this book are relevant. Who will control the questions fed into the information utility; how and in whose behalf will the answers be used? None of the guideposts suggests the slightest basis for high expectations.

There is no reason to challenge Parker's observation that "it does not take much foresight to predict that the bulk of polling activity by computer will be similar to the bulk of present opinion polling activity—namely to answer commercial or marketing research questions." And, with respect to the political surveying that will also be promoted and facilitated, Parker is equally unenthusiastic:

It should be quite evident that the kind of electronic town meeting made possible by audience response television will not bring power to the people. It will enhance the power of those with access to the sending end of the communication medium and those with power to control the wording of questions. Preelectric town meetings may have been undemocratic in the sense that they reflected the agenda of the preexisting power structure. The electric town meeting, as a result of its technical constraints, would be even less democratic because of the reduced capability for bargaining about the topics to be discussed and the wording of the questions being used. . . . the initial distribution of political power prior to conducting a poll is such that those who have the organization and resources to conduct the poll in the first place have more political power than the individual unorganized respondents . . . it should not be surprising that the people re-

ceiving the information benefit more than the people giving the information.[17]

It seems that electric technology is no more capable of transcending the institutional constraints of the prevailing social order than the less wondrous mechanics that preceded it. More pertinent than its capacity for effecting desirable social change, perhaps, is its obvious potential for further damaging the already-frail safeguards protecting democratic procedure. For example, the Cable TV Committee of the Illinois Chapter of the American Civil Liberties Union reported these less attractive potentialities of cable TV: "Without your knowledge, your cable could be tapped . . . Whoever tapped the cable could determine which programs you watched, record your transactions with banks or stores, and even monitor your conversations through your TV set . . . Five years from now if you're using a computer hookup to a library, the FBI could tell what information you've had access to . . . they could tell what underground papers you've been reading, or who you've had business with."[18]

The capacity for massive information generation that advanced technology provides permits new and curious methods of information control. Though secrecy and denial of access to information remain important means of preserving and exercising power, less recognizable techniques are also available. The very volume of data generated becomes a method of control. It is possible to lose people in mountains of data. For example, the highly publicized (and therefore quite atypical) unauthorized publication of the 4,000-page-long Pentagon Papers in June 1971 did not provide the ordinary citizen with much illumination. The raw documentation may be a lode for scholars and future Ph.D.'s, but the rapid, concise clarification of the contents of such a huge quantity of information demands an altogether different kind of informational system than that which currently exists. Most documents, of course, do not receive the attention that was paid to those highly charged records of governmental duplicity in the Vietnamese war.

Much more representative of the way information is moved, with or without the benefit of computers, is the following account of a Federal Trade Commission hearing on modern advertising practices, held in Washington in the fall of 1971. This was a highly pertinent event, in its own terms, because advertising supplies a good part of the financial support for the American informational system. Without advertising revenues, most of the major conduits of information in the country would dry up. Furthermore, as has been observed elsewhere, it is the commercial message—to secure product sales and to reinforce popular support for the system-in-general—that dominates the country's culture. It is instructive, therefore, to observe how an inquiry into the operations of this extremely important commercial and cultural industry proceeds through the information network. The weekly magazine of the advertising industry generously provided this detailed account:

The Federal Trade Commission hearings on modern advertising practices have ended, and contrary to the fears of the Cassandras, there is no lynch mob marching on Madison Avenue. There are any number of explanations for this. Was it because the ad people gave such a persuasive account of themselves? Was it because the Commission was pulling its punches? Or was it because the public never found out the hearings were taking place? [Note that the implication of these words is that a lynch mob would have been justified had there been any mass understanding of the industry's practices. According to the Advertising Age reporter] . . . there was no lynching because the public was never told anything that might have induced it to reach for a rope. [Robert R. Mullen, the Washington P.R. man who handled the hearing for the Advertising Association explains the industry's good showing in the national press] because we flooded them with material and because our witnesses dominated the hearings the reports are heavily favorable to advertisers. [But, as the AA reporter observes] there is more to it than that. For the most part the public had little opportunity to know anything about what was happening. Mr. Mullen has 1,121 clippings on the hearing through November 12. But mostly they are the identical wire service stories in advance of the hearings. There was only an occasional wire service story on the testimony as it took place and—except for the trade press—the press seats in the hearing room were empty most of the time . . . The broadcast media did even worse. A major government agency was spending 15 days to determine whether our children are being seduced by TV, *and whether 200,000,000 consumers are being "manipulated."*

But except for the fragments fed in by the occasional reports of the news services, it was "non news" for the networks and the broadcasting industry and the cameras and the tape recorders, and the network newsmen were nowhere to be seen. How's that for a performance from an industry that likes to impress us with its valiant efforts to defend "the right to know"?

The TV *news editors no doubt were making what they felt were sound editorial judgments. Yet their conspicuous indifference to the hearing could perpetuate the suspicion widely held among critics of advertising that media are more considerate of their advertisers than of the public.*

One would not want news editors to create controversies about advertising where none exists. But surely some time during those 15 days when FTC *was studying the impact of advertising, someone must have said something that was more than "non news."*[19]

This episode illustrates how the nation's informational process currently operates. There is, to begin with, information overload —fifteen days of hearings, perhaps sixty hours of testimony. In print, this is a skyscraper of documentation.[20] Who will digest it? Condense it? Simplify it? Highlight it for the millions of Americans who are daily affected by these practices? There is also the question of selectivity: which portions of the testimony will be reported? Which will be ignored? Who will make such judgments? And there is still another crucial factor in determining the informational mix. The commercial media (print, radio, and television) are all partisan to some degree because they rely so heavily on advertising revenues. Yet through these channels flows a very carefully filtered stream of information, from a preselected information universe, about advertising practices in the United States. The original information universe was by no means fully representative, because many public groups were excluded from testifying.

Information overload, therefore, is not an entirely accurate description of the condition of communications in America. There is no surplus of *meaningful* information, just as there is no surplus of good health care, adequate diet, or decent housing in the country. What we have, instead, is an ocean of irrelevant, purposeless, sensational, personal, and trivialized material. In it float bits of vital information, which move more-or-less undetected among the public relations throwaways and other forms of informational pollution.

The communications technology that has developed in recent decades facilitates the instantaneous transmission and recovery of this "informational" junk, and permits the generation of enormous quantities of additionally dysfunctional data. Since the chief users and supporters of the informational system are (1) the giant corporations, with their marketing needs, (2) the Department of Defense, with its built-in requirement for a continuous external (or internal) national security "threat," and (3) the expanding national bureaucracy, which serves both these groups and attempts to present itself as a neutral agent of the general well-being, it is to be expected that the national communications flow is hardly in the public interest, however that vague term is defined.

Prospects?

Earlier chapters have presented an account of the institutional techniques of controlling and manipulating information in the world's foremost message-producing and -transmitting society. Meanwhile, the development of new communications technology makes it possible, and even likely, that the future may be more manipulated than the already considerably managed present.

Given these actualities, it would be easy to view the immediate future as a period of inevitable massive regimentation, in both the material and cultural spheres. This could, however, be a premature judgment. There are countervailing movements stirring. Their current strength hardly matches that of the dominant forces, but they possess, all the same, certain advantages.

The emergence of a major sector of the economy engaged in a wide spectrum of informational activities calls attention to the multiplying number of "knowledge workers" in the society. As we have seen, it is precisely this educated group which is most critical of the goals and games of the system as it now operates.

This makes the tasks of the mind managers more complicated, and their success increasingly problematic, new technology notwithstanding. The knowledge labor force, though far from secure economically (it owns none of the instruments of production), does possess some leisure, some income, and, most important, some expertise. Leisure and income permit the further development of criticism, sustained by recognition of the dreadful malfunctioning of the system in general and of the part with which they are most familiar in particular. The Pentagon Papers were made available to the press, it may be noted, by individuals with sophisticated engineering and systems training. Ralph Nader recruits his "raiders" from the graduating classes of the nation's best law schools.

Is there justification for believing that the knowledge labor force will continue to increase in numbers and extend the scope of its critical outlook? There are good reasons to believe that the answer is affirmative. The growth of the knowledge labor force is a result of the historical evolution of the industrial system. Unless ecological and/or atomic catastrophe intervenes (not an insignificant qualification), there can be no return to primitive methods of production. But in the advanced industrial corporation-administered state, where monopoly in production, concentration in ownership, and anarchy in distribution and consumption prevail, the grotesque distortions of material and cultural life multiply unbearably. Signs of these crisis points have been visible for some time. The issue of so-called "inverted priorities" is characteristic of what has been aptly termed "The Sick Society."[21]

The combination of social stress and a widening pool of more-or-less educated knowledge workers and students may be expected to produce further instability. To what extent this can be cordoned off from other sectors in the nation is still unclear. There are a few indications that the malaise may be spreading to at least the younger members of the industrial working class. And there are reasons, which we shall mention briefly before we conclude, for believing that the industrial working class, young and old, may be compelled for its own protection to abandon its present support for the "system" and to adopt a vigorously critical stance.

On the communications front, information "collectives" have appeared in many parts of the country. These are generally city-based, sometimes ethnically organized community groups analyzing, criticizing, and challenging the conventional media structures. Their activities should not be minimized. The organizations engaged in this work are providing essential services to the community. Harold Lasswell has observed that "a category of particularly important information for everyone is knowledge of how he can be manipulated and thereby deprived of the degree of choice that one might have." This leads Lasswell to the view that "one does not necessarily alter one's opinion because he becomes aware of the factors that usually shape it. But if one's factor-determiners are continually brought to attention, the likelihood is improved that an individual will ask himself whether his response is, after all, satisfactory when reviewed in the light of all the information at his disposal."[22]

While all such groups taken together cannot compare in strength and resources with any *one* private communications conglomerate, the collectives' ties to popular groups and community needs give them potential vigor unavailable to the presently secure communications controllers. And they are, in Lasswell's words, trying to illuminate our "factor-determiners."

At the same time, the new communications technology, as it becomes cheaper and more available, makes it possible for relatively large numbers of individuals to become knowledgeable in media practices and routines. This may not result in immediate professional expertise, but it helps to demystify the media for a significant number of people; equally important, it begins to provide the basis for a new corps of trained individuals, capable of handling some of the now-ignored informational needs of the nation's communities.

Still another important benefit of the increasing participation in one or another form of media activity is the possibility of countering, at least in part, the powerful tendency to passivity that the modern media, as now employed, induce. Involvement by as many people as possible is an informational imperative, if this or any society is ever going to be able to create safeguards against mind manipulation of the majority by small privileged minorities.

In this respect, America today is not altogether without hope. There are untold numbers of individuals and groups outside of the mainstream working with tape recorders, cameras, videorecorders, film, music, print, radio, graphics, and public art forms. Their exclusion from the mass communication channels means that their efforts are unknown to most people. But they exist. They appear to be increasing. And, for the moment at least, their involuntary separation from the main communication conduits permits more experimentation, less homogenization, and the promise of some exciting new initiatives that may escape instant co-optation. To repeat, the involvement of many people in the media, on their own initiative and out of their own desire to communicate, is ultimately the strongest defense any society has against information control and mind management.

The evidence in this book, as well as the onrush of day-to-day events, makes it more and more apparent that all the defenses that can be mustered will be needed in the years ahead. Not only communications, but also democratic rights in general, may be in for a stormy era. In assessing the future of American capitalism, Stanford University economist John Gurley sees "powerful adverse forces" operating against the American economy. Continuing revolutionary movements abroad, intensified economic rivalries among the leading Western industrial states and Japan, and the pressure of domestic labor to hold on to its share of the income pie will be met, in Gurley's opinion, by increasing resort to state interventionism "in behalf of the capitalist class." Labor especially will suffer severe curbs.

"Some way out in the future," Gurley predicts, "a large scale revolt against the system itself," which will include many working people who are presently unmoved by social problems. "In the meantime, capitalism will survive as an increasingly directed monopoly capitalism. But many elements of democracy will not."[23]

This grim prospect is not an inevitable scenario. If Gurley's analysis is even partly correct, the system and its governors, on the defensive, will react harshly and repressively. Yet the instruments of repression, of which communications are now a vital part, are double-edged and not completely reliable.

The almost-universal ownership of radios and television sets, the large number of electronically sophisticated individuals in the country, the even larger number of people who have had considerable schooling, and the breadth of the land itself impose severe constraints on would-be total information controllers. Also, the increasing abundance of channels via cable TV, cassettes, and still-to-be discovered techniques of moving information make it extremely difficult to exercise maximum control of the message flow. To be sure, these constraints amount to little more than a prolonged holding operation, not new initiatives.

There is, however, another not inconsequential obstacle in the path of the media managers. The incongruities in the social order are great and growing. And the lopsided conditions of life in the United States are being experienced by tens of millions of people. It is difficult, therefore, for many to reconcile a trillion-dollar-plus national output with the shocking neglect of the aged, the poor, the sick, and most of the black, brown, and red minorities. Also hard for many to understand is an economic system that produces mountains of absurd goods and innumerable unjustifiable services (such as tax shelter advisors, luxury kennels for pets, and the like), while it is unable to provide doctors, dental care, adequate education, and other essential social services.

Despite deliberate efforts by the informational network to confuse or ignore these matters, the pressure of unmet vital needs intensifies, and individual consciousness cannot fail to be affected. The reality of America intrudes through TV commercials, the staged events of the Presidency, weekend sports orgies, and the exhortations of Dr. Norman Vincent Peale for more "enthusiasm."[24]

The forces that have pushed the United States to the furthest edge of capitalist development—that have produced the space program and urban decay, the inner city ghetto and suburban affluence, the car culture and transportation paralysis, the goods economy and human obsolescence—have also provided personal experiences unique to this country. These permit an increasing number of individuals, mostly young, to view the entire developmental process of a market economy from a new perspective. Questions are asked in the United States that cannot even be formulated elsewhere.

Questions alone are hardly sufficient to engage successfully the most powerful industrial structure yet created. Still, they deny to an otherwise powerful system the total mind management it is beginning to require for its survival. And as long as the system remains unchanged fundamentally, critical questions can only multiply. Already, a growing proportion of Americans no longer believe what they see and hear in the national media. Their cynicism, which now reinforces the *status quo*, could, with different stimuli, be transformed into clear-sighted opposition and political resistance.

The mind managers have worked long and arduously at their task. Their resources, made available from corporate and governmental budgets, are substantial; their successes to date, many. Yet they have not been able to prevent, in at least one portion of the population, a growth in understanding, perhaps deeper than any achieved to this time, of what the system is really all about. This should be no small encouragement to the still weak forces of liberation.

What is more, this understanding, derived from the realities of American existence, promises to be grasped by many others in the years immediately ahead. Thus, a gradually heightened consciousness, despite a more tightly controlled communications system, may develop its own means to force the social changes so desperately needed in this country today.

Notes

Introduction

1. Paulo Freire, *Pedagogy of the Oppressed* (New York: Herder and Herder, 1971), p. 144.
2. *Ibid.*, p. 145.
3. Gore Vidal, "Homage to Daniel Shays," *The New York Review of Books,* 10 August 1972, p. 12.

Chapter One

1. Alan Lomax and Norman Berkowitz, "The Evolutionary Taxonomy of Culture," *Science* 177 (21 July 1972): 238.
2. C. B. MacPherson, *The Political Theory of Possessive Individualism* (Oxford: Clarendon Press, 1962).
3. Frank Stanton, "Will They Stop Our Satellites?," *New York Times,* 22 October 1972.
4. Henry Luce, the founder of *Time, Life, Fortune, Sports Illustrated,* and other mass circulation magazines, knew otherwise. He told his staff at *Time:* "The alleged journalistic objectivity, a claim that a writer presents facts without applying any value judgment to them [is] modern usage—and that is strictly a phony. It is that that I had to renounce and denounce. So when we say the hell with objectivity, that is what we are talking about." W. A. Swanberg, *Luce and His Empire* (New York: Charles Scribner's Sons, 1972), p. 331.
5. Daniel Bell, *The End of Ideology* (Glencoe, Ill.: The Free Press, 1960).
6. Leon Eisenberg, "The *Human* Nature of Human Nature," *Science* 176 (14 April 1972): 123–124.
7. "The Social Engineers Retreat Under Fire," *Fortune*, October 1972, p. 3.
8. Eisenberg, "*Human* Nature," p. 124.
9. Paulo Freire, *Pedagogy of the Oppressed* (New York: Herder and Herder, 1971), p. 135.

10. Les Brown, *Television: The Business Behind The Box* (New York: Harcourt, Brace Jovanovich, 1971), pp. 196–203.
11. Freire, *Pedagogy of the Oppressed,* p. 137.
12. "Black Movie Boom—Good or Bad?," *New York Times,* 17 December 1972. Including Jim Brown, "Approach It As Business," and Imamu Amiri Baraka, "Modern Nigger-Toys."
13. George Gerbner, "Communication and Social Environment," *Scientific American,* September 1972, p. 156.
14. Les Brown, *Television,* pp. 59–60.
15. Robert Musel, "Through A Glass—*very* darkly," TV *Guide,* 2 October 1971, p. 12.
16. Merrill Panitt, "America Out of Focus," TV *Guide,* 15 January 1972–12 February 1972.
17. Freire, *Pedagogy of the Oppressed,* pp. 137–138.
18. Langbourne W. Rust, "Do Children Prefer Junk On TV?" *Variety,* 13 September 1972, p. 38.
19. Hedrick Smith, "Big Issues Block U.S.–Soviet Trade," *New York Times,* 12 August 1972.
20. *New York Times,* 27 July 1972.
21. Rudolph Arnheim, "Television as a Medium," Feedback #1, The Network Project, *Performance* no. 3 (July/August, 1972): 16.
22. Fred Friendly, *Due To Circumstances Beyond Our Control* (New York: Random House, 1967), pp. 27, 59–60, *passim.*
23. Martin A. Jackson, review of "The American Newsreel, 1911–1967," *New York Times Book Review,* 6 August 1972, p. 4.

Chapter Two

1. *New York Times,* 23 January 1970.
2. Paul Dickson, *Think Tanks* (New York: Atheneum, 1971), p. 7.
3. *Los Angeles Times,* 19 July 1972.
4. *Broadcasting,* 17 July 1972, p. 29.
5. *Variety,* 12 July 1972, p. 34. Also see Herbert I. Schiller, *Mass Communications and American Empire* (Boston: Beacon Press, 1971), especially ch. 4.
6. The Council for Government Communications Policy and Planning held its first meeting on April 28, 1972, under the chairmanship of Office of Telecommunications Policy Director Clay T. Whitehead. The composition of the Council supports the thesis that government communications and information policy is bound up tightly with the dominant military and private corporate power blocs in the nation. Members of the Council include: Joseph F. Donelan, Jr., Assistant Secretary of

State for Administration; Eberhardt Rechtin, Assistant Secretary of Defense (Telecommunication); James H. Wakelin, Jr., Assistant Secretary of Commerce for Science and Technology; Robert H. Cannon, Jr., Assistant Secretary of Transportation; John W. Coffey, Deputy Director of the CIA; Robert M. O'Mahoney, Commissioner of Transportation and Communications Service for the General Services Administration; and Willis Shapley, Associate Deputy Director of the National Aeronautics and Space Administration. *Telecommunications Reports* 38, no. 16 (April 24, 1972), p. 23.

7. U.S. Bureau of the Census, *Statistical Abstract of the United States, 1971* (Washington, D.C.: Government Printing Office, 1971), p. 509.
8. Nicholas Wade, "NBS Loses Branscomb to IBM," *Science*, 14 April 1972, p. 147.
9. Donald Stevenson Watson and Mary A. Holman, "Concentration of Patents from Government Financed Research in Industry," *Review of Economics and Statistics* 49, no. 3 (August 1967): 375–381.
10. Dickson, *Think Tanks*, p. 10.
11. J. E. Goldman, "Toward a National Technology Policy," *Science*, 22 September 1972, p. 1079.
12. Harry Howe Ransom, *The Intelligence Establishment* (Cambridge, Mass.: Harvard University Press, 1970), p. 8.
13. U.S., Congress, Senate, Subcommittee on Constitutional Rights, Committee on the Judiciary, "Army Surveillance of Civilians: A Documentary Analysis" (Washington, D.C.: Government Printing Office, 1972), pp. 96–97.
14. U.S., Congress, Senate, Subcommittee on Constitutional Rights, Committee on the Judiciary, *Staff Report*, April 1972, p. 4.
15. U.S., Congress, House, "U.S. Government Information Policies and Practices–Administration and Operation of the Freedom of Information Act," hearings before a subcommittee of the Committee on Government Operations, March 1972, p. 1285. Hereafter referred to as *The Moorhead Hearings*.
16. Ransom, *The Intelligence Establishment*, p. 88.
17. "Intelligence Costs for Military in '70 Put at $2.9 Billion," *New York Times*, 14 May 1970.
18. Benjamin Welles, "Nixon Reported Weighing Revamping of Intelligence Services," *New York Times*, 11 May 1971.
19. The Moorhead Hearings, p. 1033.
20. Carol M. Barker and Matthew H. Fox, "Classified Files: The Yellowing Pages" (New York: The Twentieth Century Fund, 1972), p. 15.
21. "Cost Twice as High to Conceal as Reveal," *Los Angeles Times*, 16 May 1972.
22. Robert S. Semple, "Nixon Vetoes Bill to Fund Public TV," *New York Times*, 1 July 1972.

23. "[Nixon's] actions have brought him closer to two goals of his Administration: (1) the emasculation of the Public Broadcasting Service, the modest but growing educational television network, and (2) the frustration of public affairs activities by educational television." "Politics in Public Broadcasting," editorial, *Los Angeles Times,* 25 October 1972.
24. Fred Powledge, *Public Television: A Question of Survival* (New York: American Civil Liberties Union, 1972).
25. Bill Greeley, "Deem CPB as a White House O & O Via Loomis and Other Appointments," *Variety,* 27 September 1972. See also 20 December 1972.
26. Alan Wells, *Picture-Tube Imperialism?* (Maryknoll, New York: Orbis, 1972), p. 96.
27. *Ibid.*
28. U.S., Congress, Senate, hearings before a subcommittee of the Committee on Appropriations, on appropriations to the Departments of State, Justice, and Commerce, the Judiciary and related agencies for fiscal year 1972 (Washington, D.C.: Government Printing Office, 1971), pp. 815–820.
29. John J. O'Connor, "U.S.I.A. Propaganda," *New York Times,* 1 April 1972.
30. John W. Finney, "U.S.I.A. Confirms Role In Unattributed Pamphlets," *New York Times,* 22 March 1972.

    In May 1972, the United States Senate "rejected an amendment that the Foreign Relations Committee (Senate) had put in a State Department United States Information Agency budget bill prohibiting the agency from distributing unattributed propaganda abroad." John W. Finney, "Senate, In Vote, Gives Fulbright Another In A Series of Rebuffs," *New York Times,* 26 May 1972.
31. Bernard Gwertzman, "U.S. Radio Abroad Wins Senate Test," *New York Times,* 8 June 1972.
32. James Aronson, *The Press and the Cold War* (New York: Bobbs-Merrill, 1971).
33. Gwertzman, "U.S. Radio Abroad."
34. Erik Barnouw, *The Image Empire* (New York: Oxford University Press, 1970), pp. 91–92.
35. Hillier Krieghbaum, *Pressures on the Press* (New York: Crowell, 1972), p. 210.
36. Susan Wagner, "Publishing On The Potomac: The Selling of the Government," *Publishers' Weekly,* 9 August 1971, p. 28.
37. Krieghbaum, *Pressures on the Press,* p. 210.
38. J. William Fulbright, *The Pentagon Propaganda Machine* (New York: Liveright, 1970). Quotations on page 49 are from this book.
39. Krieghbaum, *Pressures on the Press,* p. 211.
40. U.S., Congress, House, Committee on Government Operations, "Ad-

ministration of the Freedom of Information Act," report no. 92–1419 (Washington, D.C.: Government Printing Office, 1972), p. 60.
41. The Moorhead Hearings, pp. 1007–1008.
42. *Ibid.*, p. 1056.
43. *Ibid.*, pp. 1013–1014, 1047.
44. *Ibid.*, p. 3019.
45. *Ibid.*, p. 2997.
46. Representative Lionel Van Deerlin, 17 December 1971. Press release.
47. *Broadcasting*, 26 June 1972, pp. 43, 46.
48. The Moorhead Hearings, p. 3023.
49. *Ibid.*, p. 3059.
50. "CQ Fact Sheet On Committee Secrecy," *Congressional Quarterly*, 12 February 1972, p. 301. "Committee Secrecy: Still Fact of Life In Congress," *Congressional Quarterly*, 11 November 1972, p. 2974.
51. U.S., Congress, House, Committee on Government Operations, *Freedom of Information Act* (Compilation and Analysis of Departmental Regulations Implementing 5 U.S.C.) (Washington, D.C.: Government Printing Office, 1968).
52. James Reston, "Washington: The New 'War Profiteers,'" *New York Times*, 3 May 1968.
53. The Moorhead Hearings, p. 3061.
54. David Wise, "The Institution of Lying," *New York Times*, 18 November 1971.
55. Barker and Fox, "Classified Files," p. 60.
56. The Moorhead Hearings, p. 1040.
57. "Government Easing Attitude Toward Private Enterprise In Use of Federal Information," *Publishers' Weekly*, 12 April 1971, p. 27.
58. *Ibid.*
59. *Ibid.*, p. 28.
60. Professor Raoul Berger, testimony before the Moorhead Hearings, p. 3129.

Chapter Three

1. Fritz Machlup, *The Production and Distribution of Knowledge in the United States* (Princeton, N.J.: Princeton University Press, 1962).
2. *New York Times*, 10 January 1972.
3. "Education Industry Is Marketing ABC's," *New York Times*, 10 March 1972.
4. M. Marien, "Notes on the Education Complex as an Emerging Macro-System," Global Systems Dynamics International Symposium, Charlottesville, 1969 (New York: Karger, 1970), pp. 225–244.
5. David M. Shoup, "The New American Militarism," *The Atlantic* 223, no. 4 (April 1969): 51–56.

6. Clark M. Clifford, address before the National Security Industrial Association, Washington, D.C., 26 September 1968.
7. Lawrence S. Wittner, "IBM and the Pentagon," *The Progressive*, February 1972, pp. 33–34.
8. *Ibid.*
9. Mildred Benton and Signe Ottersen, comps., *Roster of Federal Libraries* (Washington, D.C.: The George Washington University, 1970).
10. "I submit that the Department of Defense, a Department which consumes 9 percent of the gross national product of our nation, a Department which employs four and one-half million Americans, has a deep obligation to contribute far more than it has ever contributed before to the social needs of our country. Justice . . . domestic tranquility . . . general welfare . . . blessings of liberty. Can it be that these essential elements of freedom are a responsibility of the rest of the United States Government, but not of the Department of Defense whose operations account for half of the total expenditures of that Government?" Clark M. Clifford, *op. cit.*, 1968.
11. Fred M. Heddinger, address before the Thirteenth Annual Summer Conference of the Pennsylvania School Boards Association, 15 July 1967. Published in the *Newsletter* of the Pennsylvania Electronics Technology, Inc. 68-3, p. 4.
12. *Phi Delta Kappan*, May 1967, 417.
13. Dr. Samuel Halperin, "Things Don't Just Happen," address before the National Industrial Association, reprinted in the *Congressional Record*, 20 February 1968, p. E 981.
14. *Publishers' Weekly*, 19 February 1973.
15. *Fortune*, May 1972, p. 149.
16. *New York Times*, 11 February 1972, p. 49.
17. Abel Green, "'Writedowns' and 'Restructuring,'" *Variety*, 5 January 1972, p. 50.
18. *New York Times*, 10 January 1972.
19. Robert W. Locke, "Has the Education Industry Lost Its Nerve?" *Saturday Review*, 16 January 1971, p. 44.
20. John Henry Martin, testimony before the Subcommittee on Economic Progress of the Joint Economic Committee, June 6, 10, 13, 1966. *Technology in Education* (Washington, D.C.: Government Printing Office, 1966), p. 151.
21. J. Myron Atkin, "The Federal Government, Big Business, and Colleges of Education," *The Educational Forum*, May 1967, p. 391.
22. Harold Howe II, "The Realities of the Learning Market," *Educational Technology*, Spring 1967, p. 39.
23. *New York Times*, 14 July 1968.
24. "Education–Government–Industry–Project Aristotle" NSIA symposium, Washington, D.C., December 6–7, 1967.

25. Fred M. Heddinger, "Will Big Business and Big Government Control R & D?" *Phi Delta Kappan*, January 1967, p. 216.
26. James A. Mecklenburger and John A. Wilson, "Learning C.O.D. Can the Schools Buy Success?" *Saturday Review*, 18 September 1971, p. 76.
27. *Los Angeles Times*, 1 February 1972.
28. *Los Angeles Times*, 28 July 1972.
29. *Publishers' Weekly*, 8 February 1971.
30. John D. Williams, "Conglomerates Cause An 'Information Loss,'" *Wall Street Journal*, 29 December 1972.
31. William F. Luebbert, "Instructional Technology, Education and Man as a Builder and User of Tools," International Symposium on Communication: Technology, Impact and Policy, The Annenberg School of Communications, University of Pennsylvania, March 23–25, 1972.

Chapter Four

1. Erik Barnouw, "Television as a Medium," Feedback #1, The Network Project, *Performance* no. 3 (July/August 1972), p. 13.
2. *Ibid.*, p. 40. George Gerbner makes the same point: "The most profound effects of communication can be found not in making sales, getting votes, influencing opinions and changing attitudes but in the selective maintenance of relatively stable structures of images and associations that stem from institutional structures and policies and that define the common perspectives of a society." "Communication and Social Environment," *Scientific American*, September 1972, p. 158.
3. Franc Shor, "Pacific Fleet: Force For Peace," *National Geographic*, September 1959, pp. 283–335.
4. *Broadcasting*, 14 August 1972, p. 39.
5. Les Brown, *Television: The Business Behind the Box* (New York: Harcourt, Brace Jovanovich, 1971), p. 59.
6. *New York Times*, 27 November 1972.
7. James Playsted Wood, *Magazines In The United States*, 3rd ed. (New York: The Ronald Press, 1971), p. 291.
8. *Ibid.*, p. 292.
9. *Ibid.*, p. 291.
10. *New York Times*, 31 July 1967.
11. "As We See It," TV *Guide*, 22 July 1972, p. 1.
12. Max Gunther, "Revolution at the FTC," TV *Guide*, 24 June 1972, pp. 27–28.
13. John C. Schwarzwalder, "Public Broadcasting Must Clean House," TV *Guide*, September 30–October 6th, 1972.
14. Merrill Panitt, "America Out of Focus," TV *Guide*, 15 January–12 February, 1972.

15. *Ibid.*
16. *Advertising Age*, 24 April 1972, p. 22.
17. *Advertising Age*, 3 July 1972.
18. Tom Buckley, "With the National Geographic on Its Endless, Cloudless Voyage," *New York Times Magazine*, 6 September 1970.
19. Frank Luther Mott, *A History of American Magazines*, vol. 4:1885–1905 (Cambridge, Mass.: Harvard University Press, 1957), p. 626.
20. "National Geographic Society Elect Key Executives," *National Geographic*, October 1967, p. 576.
21. M. B. Grosvenor, "National Geographic's Newest Adventure: A Color Television Series," *National Geographic*, September 1965, p. 451.
22. Buckley, "With the National Geographic," p. 22.
23. Mott, *History of American Magazines*, p. 625.
24. Volkman Wentzel, "Mozambique, Land of the Good People," *National Geographic*, August 1964, pp. 214–215.
25. Jules B. Billard, "Panama, Link Between Oceans and Continents," *National Geographic*, March 1970, p. 404.
26. *Ibid.*, p. 412.
27. Buckley, "With the National Geographic," p. 18.
28. Wentzel, "Mozambique," pp. 203–204.
29. Buckley, "With the National Geographic," p. 18.
30. Peter T. White, "Saigon, Eye of the Storm," *National Geographic*, June 1965, p. 862.
31. Peter T. White, "Mosaic of Cultures," *National Geographic*, March 1971, p. 329.
32. Wilhelm G. Solheim II, "New Light On A Forgotten Past," *National Geographic*, March 1971, p. 330.
33. Buckley, "With the National Geographic," p. 20.
34. W. E. Garrett, "Pagan On The Road to Mandalay," *National Geographic*, March 1971, p. 349.
35. Franc Shor, "Pacific Fleet," p. 283.
36. *National Geographic*, June 1972, cover.
37. Franc Shor, "Pacific Fleet," pp. 283, 311.
38. Thomas W. McKnew, "Four Ocean Navy In The Nuclear Age," *National Geographic*, February 1965.
39. *National Geographic*, September 1965.
40. Bill Katz and Berry Gargal, eds., *Magazines for Libraries* (New York: R. R. Bowker, 1969), p. 169.
41. Buckley, "With the National Geographic," p. 12.
42. *Fortune*, June 1972, p. 110.
43. *Nation's Business*, March 1971, pp. 46, 49.
44. Leo E. Litwak, "Fantasy That Paid Off," *New York Times Magazine*, 27 June 1965.
45. Richard Schickel, *The Disney Version* (New York: Simon & Schuster, 1968), p. 19.

46. *Ibid.*, p. 165.
47. Interim Letter to Shareholders and Employees, Walt Disney Productions, 24 April 1972.
48. *Ibid.*
49. Annual Report, Walt Disney Productions, 1971, p. 4.
50. Schickel, *Disney Version*, p. 313.
51. Annual Report, p. 28.
52. Interim Letter.
53. Dwight Whitney, "It's Practically A Branch of the U.S. Mint," TV *Guide*, 15–21 July 1972, p. 25.
54. "Disney's Live Action Profits," *Business Week*, 24 July 1965, p. 82.
55. Schickel, *Disney Version*, p. 164.
56. Litwak, "Fantasy," p. 28.
57. *Los Angeles Times*, 16 December 1966.
58. Robert Shayon, "Entertainment," Feedback #5, The Network Project, *Performance* no. 3 (July/August 1972), p. 91.
59. Annual Report, p. 21.
60. Ariel Dorfman and Armand Mattelart, *Para Leer Al Pato Donald* (Valparaiso, Chile: University of Valparaiso, 1971).
61. A. Mattelart, "Mass Media In The Socialist Revolution; The Experience of Chile," International Symposium on Communication: Technology, Impact and Policy, The Annenberg School of Communications, University of Pennsylvania, March 23–25, 1972. *Communications Technology and Social Policy*, eds. G. Gerbner, L. Gross, and W. H. Melody (New York: Wiley Interscience, 1973).
62. *Los Angeles Times*, 1 June 1972.
63. Disney once said: "I don't have any depressed moods and I don't want to have any. I'm happy, just very, very happy." J. Anthony Lukas, "The Alternative Life-Style of Playboys and Playmates," *New York Times Magazine*, 11 June 1972, p. 72.
64. Litwak, "Fantasy," p. 27.
65. M. B. Grosvenor, "Walt Disney, Genius of Laughter and Learning," *National Geographic*, August 1963, p. 158.
66. Mott, *History of American Magazines*, p. 632.
67. James L. C. Ford, *Magazines for Millions* (Carbondale, Ill.: Southern Illinois Press, 1969), pp. 57–58.
68. "*Reader's Digest* at the White House," *New York Times*, 29 January 1972.

Chapter Five

1. Harwood L. Childs, *Public Opinion: Nature, Formation and Role* (Princeton, N.J.: D. Van Nostrand Company, 1965), p. 1.

2. Marshall A. Caskey, *Polls: Critics and Proposed Controls,* Freedom of Information Center Report No. 220 (Columbia, Mo.: University of Missouri School of Journalism, 1969), p. 3. It is estimated that there are one thousand American firms that do polling. Stephen Isaacs, "The Pitfalls of Polling," *Columbia Journalism Review,* May/June 1972, p. 34.
3. Erik Barnouw, *A History of Broadcasting,* 3 vols. (New York: Oxford University Press, New York. See especially vol. 3, *The Golden Web,* 1968).
4. Paul F. Lazarsfeld, "Some Problems of Organized Social Research," in *The Behavioral Sciences: Problems and Prospects* (Boulder: University of Colorado Institute of Behavioral Science, August 1964), p. 11.
5. Paul B. Sheatsley, "AAPOR Times 21," *Public Opinion Quarterly* 32 (1968–69): 463.
6. Hadley Cantril, *The Human Dimension: Experiences in Policy Research* (New Brunswick, N.J.: Rutgers University Press, 1967), especially pp. 24, 30–31.
7. Lazarsfeld, "Some Problems," p. 11.
8. H. Cantril, *Human Dimension,* pp. 35–37.
9. George Gallup, Jr., "The Challenge of Ideological Warfare," in *Propaganda and the Cold War,* ed. John B. Whitton (Washington, D.C.: Public Affairs Press, 1963), pp. 54–56.
10. Cantril, *Human Dimension,* chs. 1, 2.
11. "Political Pollsters Head for Record Activity in 1968," *Congressional Quarterly Fact Sheet,* 3 May 1968, p. 1000.
12. George Gallup, Jr., "Image of the United States Abroad in 1969: A Report," in *The Case for Reappraisal of U.S.–Overseas Information Policies and Programs,* ed. Edward L. Bernays and Burnet Hershey (New York: Praeger, 1970), p. 18.
13. Richard L. Merritt, "The USIA Surveys: Tolls for Policy and Analysis," in *Western Europe and Perspectives on International Affairs,* ed. Richard L. Merritt and Donald J. Puchala (New York: Praeger, 1968), p. 6. Perhaps the words of Paulo Freire are applicable here: "In their passion to dominate, to mold others to their patterns and their way of life, the invaders desire to know how those they have invaded apprehend reality—but only so they can dominate the latter more effectively." Paulo Freire, *Pedagogy of the Oppressed* (New York: Herder & Herder, 1971), pp. 150–151.
14. H. Cantril, *Human Dimension,* pp. 35–40. Cantril observes, "Obviously, in a democracy such as ours, no President can successfully implement a policy he believes in unless the people are concerned about that policy and are *educated to its implications*" (p. 69). Emphasis mine.
15. Harold Mendelsohn and Irving Crespi, *Polls, Television and the New Politics* (Scranton, Pa.: Chandler, 1970), p. x.
16. Marylin Bender, "Market Research," *New York Times,* 29 August 1971.

Also see Jack J. Honomichl, "Big Business Snaps Up 22 Top Research Firms," *Advertising Age*, 20 September 1971, pp. 1, 83.

17. Richard Hodder-Williams, *Public Opinion Polls and British Politics* (London: Routledge and Kegan Paul, 1970), especially pp. 9–14.
18. Roper Research Associates, "A Ten-Year View of Public Attitudes Toward Television and Other Mass Media, 1959–1969" (New York: Television Information Office, 1969).
19. "The Perils of Polling," *Transaction* 81, no. 9–10 (July/August 1971): 8. In a subsequent issue, Burns Roper supplied this answer to a question about his organization's affiliation: "we are independent and unaffiliated. I am frank to admit, however, that we do work for clients, if that is a sin." *Transaction* 81 (September 1971), p. 14.
20. John D. Morris, "No Fault Poll Results Disputed," *New York Times*, 24 January 1972.
21. Richard Halloran, "Tactics Disputed in Fight to Win Release of P.O.W.'s," *New York Times*, 7 June 1971.
22. Cantril, *Human Dimension, passim.*
23. Report of the Standards Committee, American Association for Public Opinion Research, presented at the 1970 annual conference. (See Chapter 7, pp. 165–166.)
24. H. H. Wilson Letter from Professor to J. Edgar Hoover, *The Daily Princetonian* (Princeton University), 8 December 1970.
25. Jerome Johnston and Jerald G. Bachman, "Young Men Look At Military Service," a preliminary report. *Youth In Transition*, document no. 193, Survey Research Center, Institute for Social Research, The University of Michigan, June 1970.
26. John Herbers, "Survey Finds Fear of U.S. 'Break-Down,'" *New York Times*, 27 June 1971.
27. Richard L. Merritt, Ellen P. Flerlage, and Anna J. Merritt, "Political Man in Postwar German Education," *Comparative Education Review* 15 (October 1971): 4.
28. Milton Rokeach, "The Role of Values in Public Opinion Research," *Public Opinion Quarterly* 32, no. 4 (Winter 1968–1969): 549.
29. Mendelsohn and Crespi, *Polls, TV, Politics*, p. x.
30. *Chicago Sun-Times*, 26 June 1968.
31. Mendelsohn and Crespi, *Polls, TV, Politics*, pp. 40–41.
32. H. Cantril, *Human Dimension*, p. ix.
33. George Gallup, Jr., A *Guide to Public Opinion Polls* (Princeton, N.J.: Princeton University Press, 1948), pp. 3, 7.
34. Robert M. Smith, "Youth Found Cool to Career in F.B.I.," *New York Times*, 15 February 1972.
35. Harwood L. Childs, *Public Opinion*, p. 1.
36. Bernard C. Cohen, "The Relationship Between Public Opinion and Foreign Policy Maker," in *Public Opinion and Historians*, ed. Melvin Small (Detroit: Wayne State University Press, 1970), p. 70.

37. Kaarle Nordenstreng, "Broadcasting Research in Scandinavian Countries," in *International Studies of Broadcasting*, ed. H. Eguchi and H. Ichinole (Tokyo: NHK Radio and TV Culture Research Institute, 1971), p. 257.
38. Anthony Wilden, *System and Structure: Essays in Communication and Exchange* (London: Tavistock Publications, 1972), p. xx.
39. Alex S. Edelstein, "Ideas In Search of Methodologies In International Communications," paper prepared for Raymond B. Nixon Symposium, Minneapolis, Minnesota, April 14–16, 1971.
40. Paul Lazarsfeld, "The Discussion Goes On," *Public Opinion Quarterly* 9 (Winter 1945–1946): 404.
41. Mendelsohn and Crespi, *Polls, TV, Politics*, p. 314.

Chapter Six

1. *Advertising Age*, 19 February 1973, p. 64.
2. "What a Multinational Company Is," *New York Times*, 19 June 1972.
3. *International Advertiser* 10, no. 1 (1969): 25. An editorial review of an address by Alexander Trowbridge, president of the American Management Association and former Secretary of Commerce.
4. *The Uncertain Mirror*, Report of the Special Senate Committee on Mass Media, vol. 1 (Ottawa: 1970), p. 246.
5. James V. O'Gara, "Billings of U.S. Agencies Top $10.5 in 1971," *Advertising Age*, 21 February 1972.
6. Hugh Quinn, "Interpublic Goal of $1 Billion Agency Step Closer with C–E," *Advertising Age*, 5 June 1972.
7. *Advertising Age*, 27 March 1972. And the big American agencies get most of the business. J. Walter Thompson; McCann–Erickson; Young and Rubicam; Ted Bates & Company; Leo Burnett International; SSC&B–Lintas International; Batten, Barton, Durstine and Osborn; Ogilvy and Mather International; Doyle Dane Bernbach, and Grey Advertising were the elite ten American agencies in world marketing in 1971.
8. *Broadcasting*, 1 September 1969.
9. Edward N. Ney, president of Young and Rubicam International, said his agency had been "holding exploratory discussions in Moscow as are other major U.S. agencies." *Broadcasting*, 20 January 1969. Marsteller Incorporated, a New York agency, recently signed the first agreement for an American agency to operate in the USSR. *Los Angeles Times*, 4 January 1973.
10. "Who's Where Around the World," *Printers' Ink* (now *Marketing/Communications*) 9 June 1967, pp. 21–30.

11. Ralph Leezenbaum, "JWT: Mystical Melding of the Swinging and the Staid," *Marketing/Communications*, March 1970, pp. 22–30.
12. Philip H. Dougherty, "Advertising Agency Plans Giant Merger," *New York Times*, 12 May 1970, p. 69.
13. "The Agency Pot: Bubbling Again," *Television Age*, 14 July 1969, pp. 22–23.
14. Philip H. Dougherty, "Advertising: Dancer Joins the Foreign Set," *New York Times*, 2 March 1970, p. 52.
15. "Radio–TV Budgets Rise in Canada," *Broadcasting*, 11 May 1970, p. 56.
16. *Advertising Age*, 12 April 1971.
17. "White House Branch of J. Walter Thompson?" *Broadcasting*, 24 February 1969, p. 36.
18. *The Financial Times*, 17 November 1969.
19. "Profile of Agencies Around the World," *Printers' Ink* (now *Marketing/Communications*), 9 June 1967. Also see Flora Lewis, "Paris Ad Agency Maps Europe-Wide Campaign," *New York Times*, 8 August 1972.
20. Robert P. Knight and John D. Stevens, comps., "Articles on Mass Communications in U.S. and Foreign Journals, a Selected Annotated Bibliography," *Journalism Quarterly* 47, no. 1 (Spring 1970): 198–199.
21. Marcel Niedergang, "Double-Edged Reform for Peruvian Press," *Le Monde* (English-language weekly edition), 1 April 1970, p. 3.
22. "Profile of Agencies Around the World."
23. *Public Relations Quarterly*, Winter 1970–1971.
24. William A. Durbin, "International Public Relations," in *Current Thoughts in Public Relations: A Collection of Speeches and Articles*, eds. Malcolm M. Johnson, Thomas A. Kindre, and Will H. Yolen (New York: M. W. Lads, 1968), pp. 120–121.
25. *International Public Relations*, Gallatin International Business Aids, June 1967.
26. "Public Relations Today," *Business Week*, 2 July 1960, p. 42.
27. Fritz Machlup, *The Production and Distribution of Knowledge in the United States* (Princeton, N.J.: Princeton University Press, 1962), p. 271.
28. "Public Relations Today," p. 41.
29. Hugh C. Hoffman and Robert C. Worcester, "The International Scene: A Review of Current Practices," *Public Relations Quarterly* 13, no. 1 (Spring 1968): 12, 17.
30. "Public Relations Today," p. 42.
31. For a compilation of American PR firms in the international arena, made a few years ago (and probably not comprehensive even then), see *International Public Relations*, Gallatin International Business Aids, June 1967.

32. Harry Muller, "Latin America: How U.S. Corporate Prestige Stacks Up," *Public Relations Journal* 22, no. 6 (June 1966): 20.
33. Hill and Knowlton International, *Handbook on International Public Relations,* 2 vols. (New York: Praeger, 1968).
34. Arthur Reef, "The Satellite Beams Its First PR Program," *Public Relations Journal* 25, no. 11 (November 1969): 17.
35. T. J. Ross, "Some Observations on Public Relations Progress," in *Perspectives in Public Relations,* ed. Raymond Simon (Norman, Okla.: University of Oklahoma Press, 1966), p. 20.
36. Joseph T. Klapper, ed., "News and Notes," *Public Opinion Quarterly* 33, no. 2 (Summer 1969): 284.
37. Gallup Organization, "International Opinion Trends" (Princeton, N.J.: Gallup Organization, Inc., n.d.).
38. Arthur C. Nielsen, Sr., *Greater Prosperity Through Marketing Research: The First 40 Years of the A. C. Nielsen Company* (New York: Newcomen Society in North America, 1964), p. 34.
39. Ernest S. Bradford, comp., *Bradford's Directory of Marketing Research Agencies and Management Consultants in the United States and the World,* 1965–1966 (Fairfax, Va.: Bradford's Directory of Marketing Research Agencies, 1965–66), p. 44.
40. V. Lewis Bassie, "Question That Survey," *Illinois Business Review* 10, no. 11 (November 1953): 2.
41. Edith Marie Bjorklund, "Research and Evaluation Programs of the U.S. Information Agency and the Overseas Information Center Libraries," *Library Quarterly* 38, no. 4 (October 1968): 414. The USIA has not limited its clandestine dealings to opinion poll-taking. Secret USIA subsidies were made to Hearst-Metro–Tone News, owned half by Metro-Goldwyn-Mayer and half by Hearst Publications. Newsreels made by this company were distributed overseas and included specially inserted USIA clips in the programs. The subsidies kept this newsreel company solvent long after their competitors had folded. *Variety,* 7 May 1969.
42. It is not always simple to determine the independence of the poll-taker/surveyor, British Market Research Bureau (BMRB), for example, is a subsidiary of J. Walter Thompson. J. Walter Thompson, *Annual Report,* 1969, p. 4.
43. Robert C. Albrook, "Europe's Lush Market for Advice–American Preferred," *Fortune,* July 1969, pp. 128, 131.
44. Henry Giniger, "Westerners Filling a Technology Gap in Algeria," *New York Times,* 24 June 1971.
45. D. S. Greenberg, "Consulting: U.S. Firms Thrive on Jobs for European Clients," *Science,* 29 November 1968, p. 986.
46. *Ibid.*, p. 987.
47. Clem Morgello, "The Stock Market's Foreign Market," *Newsweek,* 27 January 1969, p. 82.

48. In Israel, the *Jerusalem Post* carries on its front page the daily Dow–Jones averages of the New York stock exchange.
49. *New York Stock Exchange Directory, 1969* (New York: Commerce Clearing House, 1969), pp. 697–98.
50. Herbert I. Schiller, *Mass Communications and American Empire* (New York: Augustus M. Kelley, 1969; paper edition, Beacon Press, 1971), especially ch. 1, "Electronics and Economics Serving an American Century."
51. Tom Sutton, "A Profits' Prophet," *International Advertiser* 10, no. 2 (1969): 6.
52. Robert Sarnoff, "Toward a Global Common Market of Communications" (Address delivered to the American Chamber of Commerce in France and the American Club of Paris, February 12, 1970).

Chapter Seven

1. Pete Drucker, *The Age of Discontinuity* (New York: Harper and Row, 1968), p. 276.
2. *Ibid.*
3. *Ibid.*, pp. 277–78.
4. Edward H. Carr, *The New Society* (Boston: Beacon Press, 1957), p. 53.
5. George Lichtheim, "What Socialism Is and Is Not," *New York Review of Books*, 9 April 1970, p. 44.
6. Raymond Williams, "Saying 'No' to Labor," *Nation*, 15 June 1970, pp. 710–12.
7. Jerry Rubin, *Do It* (New York: Simon & Schuster, 1970), p. 142.
8. *New York Times*, 5 August 1970.
9. Daniel Bell, "The Balance of Knowledge and Power," *MIT Technology Review*, June 1969, pp. 43–44.
10. *New York Times*, 5 August 1970.
11. *Los Angeles Times*, 21 September 1970.
12. Staughton Lynd, "Again—Don't Tread On Me," *Newsweek*, 6 July 1970, p. 31.
13. Theodore Roszak, *The Making of a Counter Culture* (New York: Anchor, 1969).
14. *Advertising Age*, 8 June 1970, p. 44.
15. *New York Times*, 14 and 21 November 1969.
16. "The questions I'm raising here tonight should have been raised by those Americans who have traditionally considered the preservation of freedom of speech and freedom of the press their special provinces of responsibility." *New York Times*, 14 November 1969.
17. Raymond B. Nixon testimony before the Senate Subcommittee on Antitrust and Monopoly hearings on The Failing Newspaper Act

(Washington, D.C.: Government Printing Office, 1968), pp. 2841–2842.

18. Bryce Rucker, *The First Freedom* (Carbondale: Southern Illinois University Press, 1968), pp. 140–157.
19. "The Rich Rewards of Pioneering . . . ," *Television*, March 1968, pp. 27–51.
20. *New York Times*, 21 November 1969.
21. "Rich Rewards," pp. 27–51.
22. Arthur C. Nielsen, Sr., "Greater Prospects Through Marketing Research," address before the Newcomen Society, Chicago, 30 April 1964.
23. J. K. Galbraith, *The New Industrial State* (Boston: Houghton Mifflin, 1967).
24. William Haley, "News and Documentaries on U.S. Television," in *Survey of Broadcast Journalism, 1968–69*, ed. Marvin Barrett (New York: Grosset & Dunlap, 1969), p. 60.
25. *New York Times*, 14 November 1969.
26. *Broadcasting*, 15 April 1969, pp. 23–26.
27. *Ibid.*
28. *Television Age*, 23 September 1968, p. 29.
29. *Ibid.*, p. 29.
30. *Broadcasting*, 31 August 1970, p. 57.
31. *Variety*, 19 November 1969, p. 1.
32. *Ibid.*, p. 47.
33. Edwin Diamond, *New York*, 10 May 1971.
34. *Variety*, 12 August 1970, p. 31.
35. *Variety*, 29 July 1970, p. 1.
36. *Variety*, 31 December 1969.
37. *New York Times*, 27 June 1970.
38. *Los Angeles Times*, 28 June 1972.
39. *New York Times*, 24 August 1970.
40. *Los Angeles Times*, 20 September 1970.
41. Jules Witcover, "Nixon Fall Campaign Strategy Takes Shape," *Los Angeles Times*, 24 August 1972.
42. Richard Halloran, "Tactics Disputed In Fight To Win Release of P.O.W.'s," *New York Times*, 7 June 1971.
43. *New York Times*, 20 November 1969.
44. U.S., Congress, House, Subcommittee on International Organizations and Movements, *Modern Communications and Foreign Policy* (Washington, D.C.: Government Printing Office, 1967), pp. 60–61.
45. Norman H. Nie, "Hello Central, Give Me Heaven," *University of Chicago Magazine* 62 (May/June 1970), p. 4.
46. Richard M. Freeland, *The Truman Doctrine and the Origins of McCarthyism* (New York: Alfred A. Knopf, 1972), p. 89.

47. U.S., House of Representatives, Subcommittee on International Organizations and Movements, *The Future of United States Public Diplomacy* (Washington, D.C.: Government Printing Office, 1968), p. 54.
48. Stuart Symington, "Congress' Right to Know," *New York Times Magazine*, 9 August 1970, p. 7.
49. Richard L. Tobin, "The Coming Age of News Monopoly," *Saturday Review*, 10 October 1970, p. 51.
50. *New York Times*, 23 December 1972.
51. *New York Times*, 20 December 1972.
52. *New York Times*, 23 December 1972.
53. *New York Times*, 9 October 1970.
54. E. J. Quindlen, Assistant Director for Government Preparedness, Office of Emergency Preparedness, testimony before a subcommittee of the House Committee on Government Operations. *U.S. Government Information Policies and Practices—Problems of Congress In Obtaining Information From the Executive Branch*, part 8 (Washington, D.C.: Government Printing Office, 1972), p. 2940.
55. William S. Moorhead, *Congressional Record*, 25 October 1972, pp. E 8940–8941.

Chapter Eight

1. Harold Lasswell, "Policy Problems of a Data-Rich Society," in *Information Technology in a Democracy*, ed. Alan F. Westin (Cambridge, Mass.: Harvard University Press, 1971), pp. 187–197.
2. John C. Merrill and Ralph L. Lowenstein, *Media Messages and Men*, (New York: David McKay, 1971), pp. 260–261.
3. Stuart Umpleby, "Citizen Sampling Simulation: A Method for Involving the Public in Social Planning," *Policy Sciences* 1, no. 3 (Fall 1970): 361–375. Also see "Fourth Generation Electronic Mass Communications Media," by Stuart Umpleby, prepared for the National Conference on Computer Application in Human Communication held at the University of Tennessee Space Institute, Tullahoma, Tennessee, 11–13 October 1971; and Harold Sackman, *Mass Information Utilities and Social Excellence* (Princeton, N.J.: Auerbach, 1971).
4. *Minerva: A Participatory Technology*, research proposal submitted to the National Science Foundation by The Center for Policy Research, 1 February 1971.
5. James W. Carey and John J. Quirk, "The History of the Future," in *Communications Technology and Social Policy*, eds. George Gerbner, Larry P. Gross, and William H. Melody (New York: Wiley Interscience, 1973).

6. Sackman, *Mass Information Utilities*, p. 52.
7. Morry Roth, "Pie-In-Sky Cable TV Comes Down to Earth: Hitch Now Is Capital," *Variety*, 24 May 1972, p. 38.
8. Ralph Lee Smith, "CATV: Its Impact On Existing Technologies and Institutions," in Gerbner *et al.*, *Communications Technology*.
9. Lee Metcalf, United States Senate, *Congressional Record*, 28 June 1972, S 10432–10446.
10. *Congressional Record*, 30 March 1972, pp. E 3169–3175.
11. Thomas De Baggio, "Corporate Secrecy: Issue for the Seventies," *Nation*, 28 February 1972, p. 267.
12. Robert Boguslaw, "Systems of Power and Power of Systems," in Westin, *Information Technology*, pp. 427–428.
13. George Kozmetzky and Timothy W. Ruefli, "Newer Concepts of Management, Profits, Profitability," *Information Technology* (New York: The Conference Board, 1972), p. 91.
14. Boguslaw, *Systems of Power*, p. 429.
15. Carey and Quirk, "History of the Future."
16. Edwin B. Parker, "Assessment and Control of Communications Technology," in Gerbner *et al.*, *Communications Technology*.
17. Edwin B. Parker, "On-Line Polling and Voting," in *Planning Community Information Utilities*, eds. Harold Sackman and B. Boehm (Montvale, N.J.: AFIPS Press, 1972).
18. *Los Angeles Times*, 15 March 1972.
19. Stanley E. Cohen, "Contrary To Some Fears, Madison Ave. Is Safe and FTC Hearings End," *Advertising Age*, 22 November 1971, pp. 4, 52.
20. When I tried to get a copy of the hearings, I was informed by the Federal Trade Commission that transcripts were available for inspection at the Commission's principal office in Washington, D.C. (I live in California). Otherwise, copies could be purchased from the official reporter, The Alderson Reporting Company, a *private company*, at prices that would make the entire set of hearings cost several hundred dollars.
21. Michael Tanzer, *The Sick Society: An Economic Examination* (New York: Holt, Rinehart & Winston, 1971).
22. Lasswell, "Policy Problems," p. 191.
23. John Gurley, "The Future of American Capitalism," *Quarterly Review of Economics and Business*, 12 (Autumn 1972), pp. 15–16.
24. *New York Times*, 27 November 1972. Peter Kihss, "Nixon, In Church, Praised By Peale As A Peacemaker."

Index